Why is She Acting So Weird?

A Guide to Cultivating Closeness
When a Friend is in Crisis

Jenn McRobbie

ISBN: 978-1-942646-02-0

Cover and Interior Design: John H. Matthews
Editing: Angela Lauria

Author's photo courtesy of Christa Gallopoulos
Artwork featured in author's photo by Marcela Panasiti,
Contemporary Fine Arts Gallery

Praise

We've all been there--struggling with what to say, what to do and how to act when a friend, relative, coworker or fellow homeroom mom says she has cancer. Here, with unflinching honesty, McRobbie relives the pains, triumphs and, yes, awkwardness, of navigating her friendships while facing down cancer. *Why is She Acting So Weird?* was exactly what I was in the market for--packed with thoughtful, concrete guidance based on real experience. During a crisis, it takes a village. And sometimes that village could use instructions. *Why is She Acting So Weird?* is that instruction manual.

    -Sandra Sobieraj Westfall

    PEOPLE Magazine correspondent.

"With wit, wisdom and a modern new voice, McRobbie deftly weaves a brave and heartfelt cancer memoir with a practical guide on the healing power of female friendship."

-   Jill Kargman

     New York Times best-selling novelist and creator, writer, lead actress in Bravo's new scripted series, Odd Mom Out.

"As a physician, I strive to offer my patients more than just the technical aspects of surgery and disease management. I have tried to offer care to my patients that goes beyond the disease itself. But, there is so much more. *Why Is She Acting So Weird?* has given me a glimpse into a world I have not personally experienced. It was eye-opening for me to see the importance of friendships and relationships in our lives, particularly at a time of crisis. Since reading *Why Is She Acting So Weird?*, I have changed how I view patients and value so much more the family and friend support system that is essential to healing. I have modified my approach and now encourage my patients to seek that community support."

-Hernan I. Vargas, MD
Director of the Inova Breast Care Institute
at Inova Fair Oaks Hospital

"Our tagline at the Ulman Cancer Fund for Young Adults is "Chancer Changes Lives, So Do We." It is our life's work to create a community of support for young adults, and their loved ones, as they fight cancer and embrace survivorship. *Why is She Acting So Weird?* is going to play an important role in that work. McRobbie has created an important tool for friends who are at a loss for how to help their friend cope with cancer diagnosis or other crisis. The practical guidance in this book will benefit friends and survivors alike."

-Brock Yetso, President and CEO, and Brian Satola, COO and Senior Director of Awareness and Activation, Ulman Cancer Fund for Young Adults

For The Ladies.
You know who you are.

You showed me what friendship could be.
What friendship should be.

Table of Contents

Introduction

I dreamt we walked together along the shore. We made satisfying small talk and laughed. This morning I found sand in my shoe and a seashell in my pocket. Was I only dreaming?
~ Maya Angelou

I still replay all our conversations in my head. I think to myself, "I need to call her." Then, I realize that's not really an option any more. As time goes by, the memories of our ten-plus-year long friendship get confused and jumbled up together. I remember trips together, laughing until my face hurt, serious conversations, moments of confusion and hurt, and moments of clarity and understanding. Now that I can look back on our conversations, and indeed our entire friendship, with the lens of an observer — it's so easy for me to see how she was feeling. Her caring was poured into the little gifts she prepared for me, the boxes of my favorite treats, the invitations to her house, the planning of future trips together and the look of worry on her face. She showed up even when I'm sure she didn't want to, making small talk at kid birthday parties and waiting anxiously by the phone for updates from the doctor. She was going to just *be* the "real friend" when others told me, "You'll see who your real friends are."

Our friendship started in a bar, like so many friendships that begin in our 20s. The instant connection with someone who you know is going to be your friend. Everything that followed was simple: parties, trips, marriages, vacations, jobs, kids. The defining moment of our friendship was forged in crisis. The ease of our friendship would fade when I was diagnosed with breast cancer in November 2013. Looking back now, I realize that our friendship was faltering before I got sick. But cancer changed everything.

I was 38 years old, a wife, a mom of two, and a budding entrepreneur. I was healthy. I exercised, I ate (mostly) right and there was no family history of breast cancer. I had no reason to suspect that my life was going to change so radically. Rewarded with the 20/20 vision of hindsight, I can see that being my friend after I was diagnosed wasn't easy. How easy can it be to be friends with someone who has no idea who she is any more? I was sick, frustrated, and ashamed. I wanted everything to be all right, but everything felt decidedly *not* all right. I wanted my life to stay the same, but it was changing at such a rapid pace. I was standing still while life continued around me. I had no idea whether I was going to come out the other side of this experience intact as a woman, let alone as a wife, mother, daughter, or friend. Juxtapose that confusion with visions of quickly kicking this "thing" to the curb and getting back on track with life. I spent a lot of time trying to convince myself that it would be a smooth transition from being "cancerous" to being "cancer-free."

I have such vivid memories of telling my friends what was happening with me and then instantly traveling, in my imagination, to scenes of us at 80 years old sitting on my front porch, sipping wine and cackling over how "crazy it was that I had cancer once."

Through my diagnosis, treatment and beyond, I found solace in the relationships with my friends. They were a valuable source of comfort. The well-timed card sent via snail mail. Blowing up my phone with texts designed to keep me laughing. The amazing meals prepared with such love and care. These friends rose to the occasion, veritable knights in shiny white armor. I was buoyed by their presence, their ability to be present whether I was angry, sad, hurting, sulking, or happy. At a time when I could barely accept myself, their love and tenderness saved me from dark despair.

But there was pain too. And not just the physical kind. Some of the pain was temporary, a mere headache in a lifetime of interactions. Ill-timed comments on social media. Impersonal "I'm not worried, you got this" comments punctuated by long silences. Just like that random headache, those people faded from sight and mind quietly. By the time I noticed they were gone, I'd already moved on to the next set of experiences.

The worst pain came in the form of friendships that lingered well after their expiration. Like a migraine, we would cling to each other despite the searing pain and heat and frustration. They would offer noncommittal support. I would pull away and not keep them informed. Their sense of entitlement to knowledge about everything happening with me interfered with my new found desire for privacy. All I wanted to do was close my eyes and sleep off the experience. I just wanted it to go away. Then, seemingly without warning, the pain stops. The relationship goes away. The memory of the pain lingers and you walk around gingerly waiting for it to return. It doesn't. They don't.

What I've come to understand, now, is what made some friends achieve legendary friend status, while others faltered or failed. I have a deep and emotional understanding of the unexpected burden my friends bore during my sickness. They wanted to help, but they didn't want to get in the way. They wanted to be serious about my condition, but they wanted to see me laugh. And some just didn't want a thing to change between us.

I'm convinced, now, that each and every friend did everything they could think of to ease my burdens and my journey through this unknown. And sometimes, it still wasn't enough for me. I wanted help, but didn't know how to ask. I wanted to be serious about my treatments, but I so desperately wanted to laugh. I wanted to share how much I was changing and how confusing it all was, but I didn't want it to change our friendship. Everything was so weird. Top that off with my own feelings of wanting to be a good friend. Of not wanting to interfere in *their* daily lives. Of not wanting to "drag them down" with me and mine.

Today, I don't appear that different on the outside, aside from my newly curly hair. On the inside, however, things have shifted radically. I am a different person now. I used to hate talking on the phone — with anyone — but now I'll readily call on folks just to check in with them. When I hear of a plight facing someone I know, I immediately spring into action instead of merely trying to placate with vacuous promises of "anything I can do?" I reach out to the people around me now. I lean on them. I listen to them. I talk to them openly about my pain, my frustration, my weakness. And I don't hide it all behind walls of positivity any more. I trust my friends to handle whatever I hand them, because they can. They have. They will.

I didn't expect a cancer diagnosis would lead me to so closely scrutinize my friendships. Maybe analyzing my friendships was an easy way for me to take my mind off of what I was facing, but I don't think it's that simple. I focused on my friends and the relationships I have with them because they are so important. Cancer led me to a newfound clarity around what it takes to be a friend to someone in a crisis, and why some folks seem to rise to the occasion, while other friendships crumble and fade.

In talking to my friends, they have admitted to me that it was really difficult to know what to do or say. I was acting so weird (well, for me anyway) and my friends were left trying to figure out why. I didn't know how to tell them what I needed and they didn't know how to react. *That's* what this book is really about. It's about why I was acting so weird. I want to share, with you, the things that brought me comfort. And the things that brought me pain. I want you to see yourself in my friends.

The crisis you and your friend are facing may be an unexpected one, like a serious illness or losing a job. Or, it may be one that's been a long time in the making, like a divorce or the failing of a business. The type of crisis is irrelevant. What's relevant is the total upheaval. Now that I'm on the other side of that chasm, I want to show you what life looks like after the dust settles and you and your friend get a chance to breathe again. I want you to see just how integral *you* are to your friend in crisis, just as my friends were to me. How integral friends are to helping each other deal with a crisis.

Mostly, though, I want you to understand why your friend is acting so weird. I want you to feel empowered to be the best friend possible. I know that's what you want too. That's why you picked up this book.

Walking with a friend in the dark is better than walking alone in the light.
~Helen Keller

Chapter One:
Offering More Than
Moral Support

Fear makes strangers of people who would be friends.
~ Shirley MacLaine

I know that the first thing you want to know is how to take care of your friend. You're scared and, frankly, feeling pretty clueless about what to do to help. The thing is, without *this* chapter, you won't be in a position to help your friend as effectively as you would like. I know you'll be resistant to doing anything for yourself right now, but bear with me, please. This is important. If my friends had known this information going into my own crisis, then we would have saved ourselves so much heartache and pain.

Building A Support System For Yourself

Despite relying primarily on my husband, Craig, for my emotional support at the time of my crisis, I considered my two best friends, Amy and Tess, a major part of my support system.

They offered me levels of support different than what Craig offered. I didn't do much of anything without telling them about it. I would call each of them individually before an appointment to discuss my fears and concerns. Then, we'd be on the phone again after each appointment. I felt like I wasn't a good friend if I didn't contact each of them individually to keep them "in the know." I'm not going to lie, it was frustrating for me to have to recount stuff over and over again. I was having such a hard time processing the information I was receiving on a daily basis, that having to recount it repeatedly was painful.

Of course, I suspected they were talking to each other quite a bit about me as news rolled in from each appointment. This was most evident the few times one of them would say to me, "Oh, I'm all caught up on your last appointment" at the start of a conversation. Those words were such relief to me! It made me so happy knowing that I didn't have to relive and relay the information over and over again. It relieved so much stress: the stress of feeling like I wasn't including them in my life, the stress of making sure they each were ok, the stress of being the bearer of bad news all the time. It made me so happy that they each had someone to hang out with that wasn't bogged down in fright all the time. It made me so happy that they had each other. In fact, nothing made me happier.

If you get nothing else from this book, please understand that it is ok for you to get support for yourself through your friend's crisis. In fact, you are going to need support to get through this crisis. And you are going to resist getting that support because, well, you're not the one in the middle of a crisis after all. Why in the world would you need support? Your life is pretty good right now, thank you very much. You don't need anything. Your friend, on the other hand? She is in desperate need of help. So, you should be building a support system for her, right? Why would you be wasting time on yourself?

Time spent getting yourself centered, in light of this crisis, is not selfish. It is not time wasted. If you are in pain or worried or stressed about *her*, then it is *your* responsibility to tend to that pain, worry or stress. You also must realize that it will take some time and energy to figure out your own support plan, especially if the friend-in-crisis is the person who you would normally turn to when you had a grievance about your own life. You'll close off part of yourself for fear of adding to her burden.

I won't lie to you: you are right in feeling like all your burdens do not need to be placed on your friend. Frankly, that's true, crisis or not. By putting a system in place for facing your own demons head on, you will be better able to provide your friend with the focused care she needs. Don't isolate yourself from the person you want to help the most because you're being stubborn about getting your own emotional needs met. Look, it's normal to be scared for your friend, or worried you are doing the wrong things, or frustrated she isn't following through on medical advice. But, whatever you're stressing about? Well, that's about you. As weird as it sounds, you are going through a crisis too! The first step is facing up to the sad fact that this isn't just happening to your friend. It's happening to you too. Acknowledging that means you need to build a support system to help you grieve and cope.

Obviously, your friend is pretty much off-limits for discussions about how you feel about her crisis. So, that likely means your current support system is going to change. And change is hard! I know you want to do things to help your friend, but getting yourself to a place of calm acceptance is, in fact, doing something pretty major for your friend. If your friend feels for you the way I feel for my friends, then your friend wants to know that you are fine. Creating that knowing is the most significant way you can help. Knowing that you are not in need of support frees your friend to expend their scant energies on themselves.

What happens if you don't set up a good support system for yourself? You end up floundering. You end up doing things with the belief that they are "for your friend" but the intent is really to ease your own mind that you are "doing something."

This is making the crisis about you, instead of about your friend.

You definitely deserve to have attention and care. But, that attention and care should not be disguised as helping anyone else but yourself. There is no shame in doing things for yourself, especially if they make you feel good! When you feel good, you can help others feel good. Plain and simple.

This happened to a neighbor and good friend of mine, Carrie. At the time I was diagnosed with cancer, Carrie had been bombarded with bad news from all sides. Her husband's uncle was diagnosed with cancer. Then, one of her oldest friends had just been told their six-month-old baby had cancer. My diagnosis was the third cancer tragedy to hit her in the face. She was reeling from the punches. The people around her, that she loved and cared for very deeply, were all facing life threatening situations.

Carrie pestered me about accepting help from her. When I told her, quite honestly, that there was nothing I needed *yet*, she didn't know what to do. I could see the reaction on her face. She didn't like that one bit. In an attempt to be "doing something" to help, Carrie set up calendar on a caregiving website and called the calendar "Our Neighborhood Cares." She sent out invites via e-mail to a bunch of people in our friend circle and sent me a note, "I set this up for you. Log on when/if you feel like directing us in our energies for supporting you."

Sounds awesome, right? Well, I didn't think so. I had no clue what kind of support I needed yet...so her actions made me mad. I didn't want meals delivered to us. I didn't want people going out of their way to do stuff for us. I didn't want to have a whole website dedicated to caring for the "poor McRobbie family with all their tragedy and pain and sadness." And I sure as hell didn't want to manage how that care taking was going to happen. Of course, none of this was what Carrie was thinking when she set up this site. She was thinking, "I'm really sad this is happening to Jenn so I will do something." And this is what she chose. The error was in doing something that was aimed at me. I wasn't interested or even able to process that I was going to be in need of a tremendous amount of support at that point. What I needed, at that time, was for Carrie to engage in some serious self-care. She had her own turmoil to deal with in the wake of all these cancer diagnoses. Instead of caring for me directly, I needed her to give me a good example of how much you should care for yourself when you are faced with anger and angst and scariness in your life. I needed her to direct her energies toward another outlet while I figured out how this was all going to work. So, in jumping the gun, she might have made herself feel better about things, but it made me feel worse.

As part of this process of creating a support system for yourself you'll need to be very honest in identifying the level of your relationship with your friend. In April 2013, the Los Angeles Times printed an op-ed piece entitled: "How Not to Say the Wrong Thing."[i] The gist of the article is that the people we know can be formed into relational concentric circles around us. At the center most circle is the person in crisis. In the next ring is the next closest person — usually spouse, or kids or immediate family. Then, in the next ring is other family, or really close friends. And the circles just keep getting larger and farther away from the center person until they finally terminate at "totally random people." The general rule of thumb is, in the authors' words, "Comfort In, Dump Out." In other words, you should only offer comfort and support to those in rings that are smaller than

your own. If you have something bad to say —
either about your friend or about the crisis —
you should only offer those comments to people
on your own ring or rings larger than yours.]

I definitely feel like this relationship diagram
oversimplifies relationships. However, it has
significant merit. The biggest problem with this
theory is: most people don't know on which
ring they sit! I'll even go out on a limb and say
that *most* people misjudge where they fall in the
rings, assuming they are on a smaller ring than
they are. Setting aside those logistics, though,
the "Comfort In, Dump Out" theory is sound.
Rather than throwing your hands up in
frustration, spend some time looking for clues as
to where you fall in this "Ring Theory." Start
with some general questions about your
relationship:

1. Am I the first person called, outside of
   family, when updates occur?
2. When we do talk, do our conversations
   last more than 5 minutes?
3. When we do talk, does my friend talk
   more than I do?
4. Is my friend revealing inner thoughts to
   me?

5. Do I have direct contact with my friend's family?
6. In the past, have I taken my problems to this friend?
7. In the past, have I confided many secrets to this friend?

The more YESes you have, the closer you are to the inner circle. Taking the time to figure out where you are will save you from putting your foot in your mouth when you really intend to extend a helping hand. The other beauty of realizing which circle you are in: you gain an understanding of who is *your* potential support system. If the ring you are on now became the center ring, who are the people on the rings surrounding you? Now you know who you can talk to about your friend's crisis, without feeling like you're going to burden your friend.

Step Out Of Your Shoes

On the day that I got my diagnosis, I remember calling Amy and Tess. I don't remember who I called first. I just remember being so confused because their responses were so different. Tess was in complete shock. Her little sister had just beat breast cancer a few years before. It was still fresh for her. She cried. She was angry (at cancer, not me). She told me "we're going to beat this." And rather than sound hollow, the battle cry made me feel loved and held. I remember thinking that we were in this together, Tess and me.

Amy was silent. Then, she launched into information gathering mode, "Ok, what's next? Who do you call? When is that? What time? Do you want me to be there? What does that mean?" By the time I got off the phone with her, my head hurt. I was so sick of talking, of answering questions, and most importantly — of not having any answers! I understand that her questions came out of fear. Fear of losing me, fear of change, fear of the unknown. Cancer is a scary thing! But in that fear, she pushed me away. Instead of drawing me near, cocooning me in kindness, she embraced information. Information was what *she* needed, what would have made *her* comfortable had she been in my shoes. But, she wasn't in my shoes. She was standing firmly in her own. And as a result, she couldn't see that all *I* needed was a simple verbal embrace. I needed the "we got this" battle cry. Instead of feeling like we were in this together, it felt like Amy was standing near me, but not by me. And that's just not where comfort and solace reside.

The thing is, it is really hard to know what another person wants if they don't tell you outright. And I'm the first to admit that I didn't tell Amy what I needed. Hell, I didn't even know what I needed. So, she was left to her own devices. We had never really been through a true crisis together before. Yes, break ups and screw-ups and such — but not a life and death sort of crisis like cancer. So, we had no framework to work within. As a result, she fell into patterns of behavior that would make her feel better.

Now, I can see that her pain, her fear, got in the way of her ability to offer me the love and support I needed at that moment. She was so all consumed with her own grief that she couldn't remove herself from it. My guess, though, is that the moment she clued into the fact that she was grieving, she felt guilt. Guilt that she was feeling sad, when she wasn't the one that was sick. Guilt that she was healthy, when I wasn't. Guilt that she was one of my best friends, and yet couldn't figure out how to lift my burdens. You name the guilt, I'm sure she had it. And that guilt got in the way of our friendship.

I remember, very distinctly, a conversation where Amy said to me, "I haven't had to deal with cancer either, so I don't know what to do. I'm doing the best I can." I thought that statement was about her turning the conversation to herself and away from me. It felt like her not knowing what to do was more important than my being scared and lost. To me, it was a statement that divided us instead of bringing us together to say, "We are in over our heads. This is new. Let us tackle this together." And therein lay the acute difference between how we both were handling my crisis: I versus We.

Step Into Her Shoes

If you can, for a moment, step outside of your shoes. Pad across the floor barefoot. Feel the cold under your feet. Then, step into your friend's shoes. Feel how weird they are. How the size is *not* just right — because the shoes aren't yours. Feel the difference. From this viewpoint, look down at your friend's shoes and think to yourself, "What does she need from me?" I believe the answer will be clearer than you might expect. Can you see that what you want someone to do for you may not be the same as what your friend needs? This realization is a huge step in being able to offer your friend the support and comfort she so desperately needs from you.

With your friend's shoes on, let your intuition guide your actions when "doing" things for your friend. For example, I had an acquaintance show up at my house well after dark with her daughter and a gift bag in tow. We weren't expecting visitors, and were in the middle of our nighttime routine. I was in the middle of chemo, so I was tired, bald, and not very social. When the knock on the door came, I opened the door to see this acquaintance standing there with an expectant look on her face. Next to her was a little girl that was clearly unhappy with the stop at my house. The acquaintance launches into a story about how she just found out about my cancer and how sad she is and how she really wanted to just do something really nice for me. All the while, I'm thinking to myself, "What is your name again?" I mean, I recognized her face, but I could not, for the life of me, figure out her name. The context just wasn't right. She'd never been to my house before, and I had never met her daughter, so I didn't even recognize the little girl standing with her. I was downright confused. We had a brief stilted conversation where I felt obligated to update her on where I was in my treatment and how I was feeling. But it felt forced. And uncomfortable. After she left I realized, thankfully, she'd put a card in the gift bag with her name on it. But, given that our relationship was not very close, I felt compelled to find a way to thank her. Which meant I spent most of the next day finding out her last name and reacquainting myself with just how the heck I knew her. I was expending energies that, frankly, I had little of at the time.

Had she put herself into my shoes, just for a moment, she might have realized that knocking on my door, unannounced, in the dark, with a story about how horrified my diagnosis had made her wasn't the best course of action. Her intent, clearly, was to give me a ray of sunshine in what she figured was probably a pretty bad day. A moment in my fuzzy socks might have told her that a note, or a gift left at my door step might have been a more appropriate gesture, because it wouldn't have necessitated me interacting with her out of context and at an unusual time of day.

The hardest part about acknowledging your own sadness and shock about your friend's situation is how selfish it feels. I wish I could take away that feeling for you, because it is decidedly not selfish to take care of yourself at any time in your life. In fact, your friend in crisis expects it. And if they don't, it's only because they don't understand yet that you taking care of yourself is putting you in a better position to help them. If you can gently acknowledge what you are going through, you and your friend will be stronger and better able to cope with the challenges that are sure to arise in the future. You'll be able to face this crisis together instead of as divided individuals. In fact, you'll be calm and grounded for that moment when your friend needs you most: when she breaks down and really shows you her grief.

Chapter Two:
Making Space For Your
Friend's Grief

The friend in my adversity I shall always cherish the most. I can better trust those who helped to relieve the gloom of my dark hours than those who are so ready to enjoy with me the sunshine of my prosperity.
~ Ulysses S. Grant

Once I was diagnosed, I sat at Amy's kitchen table with her to discuss the big "C." I tried to use the word cancer prolifically so that I'd be used to the sound of it. We each huddled over our coffee. I remember acting very matter-of-factly, "I don't know what all this means, but this is what the doctors say..." I wasn't very emotional. I didn't know how to be. I was numb. The more I talked about my diagnosis and what was to come, the more panicky I would get. In order to stay in control and not lose my head, I stuck with the facts. It was like I was reciting the Gettysburg Address.

As a result, I think, of my holding back, I remember feeling very separate from her. We were sitting on opposite sides of a circular table, which is hard to do since a circle doesn't even have sides. I felt distance. There were leagues between us — a chasm that I did not know how to cross. I don't know what she was feeling at the time, because I didn't ask. And that probably explains why I had no idea where she was coming from when she said to me, "I can't lose you." I nodded, feeling the same way. I can't lose her either. I can't lose me either. I just can't lose! But she continued on, "I don't think you're going to die. You're going to beat this. I mean, I can't lose *this*," she says as she gestures back and forth with her hand, trying to span the distance between us. I don't know if I remember the conversation exactly as it happened, or if I'm making up some of the words. But, the gist is there. She was telling me something deep and dark inside her: she was afraid of losing my friendship.

At the time, I did not really understand what she meant. Why would she lose my friendship?

Looking back now, with dry eyes and a softer heart, I get it. I understand that she was afraid because our friendship had been a little strained before all this diagnosis stuff happened. I understand that she felt the chasm I felt. I understand that she was trying to tell me, in her own way, that she loved me. I loved her too. So, in that moment, the phrase, "I can't lose you," became a battle cry to me. I knew I was being called to wage a war against cancer. In fact, that was easy for us both to understand. But within that war, I was being called to fight an important battle I am only now understanding: the "friendship preservation" battle. This seemed so much more predictable than cancer. I remember, so distinctly, the physical reaction I had to hearing those words. I sat up straighter, I sucked in my stomach, I clenched my pectoral muscles together. I was, literally, steeling myself — hardening my interior and exterior — to any change in our friendship. Here I sat, feeling like my body had betrayed me. I could not, in turn, become the betrayer by driving away one of my best friends.

Now, I realize that the "friendship preservation" battle was far more complicated and difficult than fighting cancer. With cancer, I had a team of experienced doctors to lead me into each phase. They knew what I could expect. They knew what to warn me about. They knew how to lead. Amy and I, however, had never crossed this territory before. So, I prepared to fight for my friendship like I would fight for anything — with focus and control. The thing is, I had no control over anything at this time. I was stressed. I was fearful. I didn't know what to do.

When you are stressed or scared, how do you react? Do you continue to push the envelope, fighting whatever is causing you pain? Or do you avoid the pain altogether, taking flight either physically or mentally? The "fight or flight" stress responses are pretty much a standard part of the human vernacular these days. They were first coined as terms to describe stress response in 1915 by Walter Bradford Cannon.[ii] In short, Cannon's research showed that if we are faced with a threatening or stressful situation, our instincts will drive us to either "fight" or take "flight." That means we either armor up in preparation for a threat (fight) or we run away to avoid conflict (flight).

I'm sure we all have stories about how either fighting or flighting saved us from some fearful encounter.

I think, however, that there is another response that doesn't get as much discussion in our culture: the freeze. In the animal kingdom (which we are a part of, whether we want to admit it or not), some animals play dead when confronted by a predator in the hopes that they can convince the predator they are dead or simply not a good meal. Peter A. Levine explained the human version of freezing very well in his book, *Healing Trauma*:

> We humans use the immobility response — frozen energy — regularly when we are injured or even when we feel overwhelmed. Unlike the impala, though, we tend to have trouble returning to normal after being in this state. The very feelings that we need to access in order to help us steer ourselves back to the present are, in effect, numbed-out.[iii]

So what does this have to do with what happened between me and Amy? Well, it's pretty clear that I was "armoring up" to fight a two prong battle; one battle against the loss of my health and the other battle against the loss of my friendship. What I also know about myself is that this news — this being pushed to fight — well, it was stretching me too thin. My friend's desire to keep things just as they were, instead of being receptive to change, placed me in the position of needing to evaluate the threat of losing my friendship at the same time as I was evaluating the threat of cancer. I was overwhelmed.

I couldn't do it all. I had to divide and conquer. In my mind, I didn't have a choice regarding my health — that battle needed to be fought and won. So, I had to freeze my friendship in place. I had to hold things as they were during that place and time. I had to maintain the status quo. I did not have the capacity to fight two battles at once. I cared so much about our friendship that the only response I had was to numb myself to the emotions that were coming up regarding our friendship. So, I just shut down all my emotions because I couldn't tell which ones were linked to which battle. By doing that, I closed myself off from emotions that might have helped me cope with *either* battle. In effect, I ended up waging a battle with myself too.

The issue with numbing emotions is, as Levine alluded to in the quote above, that we need our feelings — our emotions — in order to cope with stress. In the book *The Language of Emotions* by Karla McLaren, she states: "Emotions are messages from our instinctive selves…If we ignore and repress an emotion, we won't erase its message — we'll just shoot the messenger and interfere with an important natural process."[iv] So, in my fear, in my overwhelmed state, I was deprived of the single most important thing that would help me cope — my emotions. This was, in no way, Amy's intent! She wanted to let me know that I was loved and cherished. I know that now. But, my psyche was very delicate at that time. The added emotional strain was too much for me to deal with. As a result, I couldn't cope well with either my cancer or the potential loss of my friendship.

You may be wondering what's so bad about wanting to preserve the friendship as it existed. My initial response, obviously, is that there was nothing at all wrong with keeping things just as they are. But, that is not an acknowledgment of the truth we were facing. When you are faced with a crisis, you — and the people around you — are going to change. It's part of the natural cycle of life. Things would be boring if we always stayed the same. Change is hard. And it's not always welcome. But, in that change, we have a golden opportunity to grow beyond measure. Amy and I, we had a chance to witness our friendship blossom into something even bigger and deeper than it had been before. Instead, we turned our back on the opportunity in order to stand steadfast and still, uncertain and apart.

I ended up finding deep solace and an ability to express my emotions in a place I never expected to: the middle of a rock concert. There were long standing plans between another of my friends, Christine, and me to go see P!nk in concert. I was so excited. Not only had she scored amazing seats, but I had always wanted to see P!nk perform. Once I was diagnosed, Christine gave me an out, "Jenn, if it's too much, it's fine!" We talked, in depth, about the concert and ultimately I decided I should still go. I didn't want to miss the opportunity of a lifetime. I didn't want my life to stop as a result of my sickness. And, most of all, I wanted to forget for a little bit and have some fun.

Christine had four tickets to the concert. So, she invited two other women that I hadn't met before. I was a little nervous to be around people that I didn't know well, in light of how emotional I'd been over the last several weeks. Christine assured me that it would be ok. She even told one of the ladies, with my approval, about what was going on with me so that it wouldn't be a complete shock if it came up in conversation.

Everything was going well. The seats were amazing. The music was even better. The group was fun and funny and I felt myself loosening up. It was such a relief to sing, shake in my seat and drink beers just like I would have before cancer. And then, one of P!nk's most popular songs at the time comes on. The song was called "Fucking Perfect."[v] In the song, she sings about making some wrong turns and making mistakes. The refrain then begs the listener not to feel anything other than perfect. She ends the song by telling the listener that they *are* perfect. Of course, upon hearing this song, I'm reduced to a pile of tears.

Now, I've always been a lyrics kind of girl. And these lyrics? Well, they hit me hard. They hit me right in the center of my pain. I did *not* feel perfect. I felt damaged. I felt scared. I felt unsure. And here was this amazing artist singing right to that insecurity, urging me to believe that I was perfect. The tears started rolling out unbidden and I could barely catch my breath. Looking back, I can still remember that moment as if it was happening right now: I look to my right and to my left and I realize that I am sitting next to two women I had never met before this night. Sure we'd been having an awesome time right up until that moment, but now I felt them staring at me. I felt their concern. I immediately felt like a fool. I didn't want to ruin their concert experience with my petty emotions! What was I thinking? But I just couldn't control the tears. They were becoming more like sobs now. As I continued to look back and forth between these women, and at Christine, who was one more seat way, I suddenly stopped worrying about feeling like a fool. I stopped worrying about ruining their concert experience. All I felt was their concern and a calm reassurance. It was emanating off of each one of them. These women, who I didn't even know before this day, sat with me, silently observing and holding me and my emotions. The tears began to subside. And, weirdly, I began to feel much better. I was looking into the faces of two strangers and feeling more held, more supported, than I ever had before.

What's even crazier about this experience is that looking back, I can actually access the calm and quiet that these ladies exuded that night. It's almost like they infused me with the ability to reach deep within myself and find solace in big emotions. I've thought a lot about the difference between this experience and the experience at Amy's kitchen table. I wanted to attribute it to their age, to their experience, to their surprise, to dumb luck. I haven't seen those ladies since that night, but as I moved through diagnosis into treatment and beyond, I've been able to gain an understanding about how they were able to support me during a very tough time. And it is simple, really. They waited. They observed, silently, without trying to fix me or my tears. They filled the time with me, without reaction, other than to offer a kind pat on the back and a tissue. They held space for me and my emotions, without judgment.

We hear the phrase "holding space" a lot these days. It was neither something I understood nor something I was interested in doing for others. After this experience, however, and many more that followed with different folks during and after my cancer crisis, I began to understand what all the hoopla is about. At a basic level, it's about letting your loved ones be themselves. It's about allowing your loved ones let their guard down. It's about letting your loved ones be loved. It's about putting aside your own responses or reactions until the emotion passes.

Before I experienced this first hand, "holding space" seemed like an awfully passive way of dealing with emotion. It certainly did not feel like a way to help a friend ease their pain. It felt *inactive*. It felt *powerless*. But, now that I've experienced it directly, I know that the opposite is true. It requires true strength and fortitude to sit with your friend while her heart melts out onto the floor. It is a conscious act of caring. It is sometimes the only way you can actually help your friend when she is in the middle of an emotional tide.

And while all of this is very hard to do, the best part is that you don't have to do it for very long. Holding space allows the person expressing emotion the time to process what they are feeling. Amazingly, it only takes the human body and brain about 90 seconds to process any given emotion.[vi] At least on a chemical level. So, tell me, is there anything you think you cannot do for 1.5 minutes? No matter how uncomfortable or awkward you may feel at your friend's outburst of emotion, just know that you only need to lend support and hold space for a mere 90 seconds! The best part is that the effect of this safe bubble of space continues to provide comfort to your friend, even when you aren't there to hold them.

Before I learned all this, I assumed that the difference between providing a supportive environment for emotional release and providing a non-welcoming environment was how close you were to the people you were with. I'm not talking proximity, but rather how well you knew the people you were with. I figured that the better you knew someone, the easier it would be to express emotion in front of them. To me, this perception of ease was what I believed would help turn an emotional moment into a bonding one. What I've since learned (and hope to impress upon you), however, is that it is not about how close you are to the person in crisis! As I experienced, you can be a virtual stranger and still provide a loving, supporting, safe environment for the expression of emotions. To do that, though, definitely requires a specific skill: to be still, acknowledge the emotional reaction, and wait for it to pass.

Practicing this skill is going to be uncomfortable, in the beginning. As a society, we do not tend to reward passivity. But, you can't think about this as being passive. It is a new way of being interactive with your friends. The greatest gift you can give your friend is to remain present while they express and feel through their emotions. They will feel loved and supported and you will know that you are doing the most supportive thing that can be done at the moment. Then, once the emotion passes, you can move on together.

So, how do you hold space for a friend when you've never done it before? If you type "how to hold space" into Google, you get a plethora of articles that give you guidance and advice. All of that advice is good, if you have an innate understanding of what holding space actually *is* in the first place! A lot of the advice, at least to me, seems so amorphous: let go, be grounded, open your heart, be conscious. Those all sound great and they *do* lead you to that place of calm acceptance where you can just be present with your friend and their emotions. However, I find it all so confusing. Add to that confusion the experience of being thrust into a complicated emotional outburst, and you're not going to remember diddly-squat. Sure, you can practice a multi-layered, multi-step process for calming yourself down so that you can then exude that calm for your friend. And I encourage that. But, in the meantime, there are really only four things that I recommend you do when a friend needs you to hold space for their emotions:

Close Your Mouth

It's so easy when you see someone expressing a strong emotion to try and placate them with words. If it's fear you say, "don't be scared." If it's anger you say, "don't be angry." If it's sadness you say, "don't be sad." The problem with these statements is they are really designed to ease your own discomfort with the emotional display. You're telling your friend to stop doing what they are doing. But, as McLaren says, "When we express our emotions, we hand them over to the outside world where we hope they'll be noticed, honored, and transformed."[vii] The first and most effective way you can notice and honor your friend's emotions is to stay silent so that you can honestly experience the emotion with your friends.

Open Your Ears

Once you are silent, you will be able to listen more intently to what your friend is saying. If your friend is actually talking or expressing their emotion with words, then you will be able to help them specifically address the root of the emotion when they are not in such a heightened state. McLaren tells us: "Your emotions don't disappear when you're not feeling them; instead, each of your emotions moves through you at all times, and each one endows you with specific gifts and abilities."[viii] Truly holding space for your friend can be followed later by a dissection of the emotion, and what that emotion is trying to teach your friend about how they are feeling. If you do not listen, however, you will not hear what the emotion is really about.

This still applies if your friend is not using words to express their emotion. If they are only sobbing, for instance, and cannot catch their breath, then you may listen to the tenor and strength of the cries. You can observe their body language to try and glean what might have triggered the emotion. Remember, it only takes around 90 seconds for us to chemically process emotions. All of the information you gather about your friend will only help you and your friend to forge ahead once the emotion has passed.

Open Your Hands

Body language is an important part of any relationship. And even though your friend seems so mired in her emotions that she can't seem to notice that you're in the middle of the grocery store (where, apparently, emotional outbursts are discouraged), she knows you are there. She is looking to you for support and hoping not to find judgment. Interestingly enough, hiding your hands may give others the perception that you are not open and honest.[ix] So, instead of needing to tell your friend how you feel, you can show them by opening your hands and holding them with your palms up. You don't have to touch your friend, unless that feels like an appropriate thing to do. Your hands may sit on your lap with the palms generally open and up. Your arms may hang at your sides with your palms facing your friend. Either way, this stance will signal that you are trustworthy and have nothing to hide.[x] That feeling will, in turn, transfer to your friend as she is processing her emotion. She will know that you are waiting and holding a safe space for her, no matter what emotion she has expressed or needs to express.

Breathe

Although breathing is an automatic function of our bodies, control of your breath can be used to infuse calm in any situation. Imagine a time when you were getting ready to do a really difficult task. What did you do right before you dove in? You probably took a deep, long breath. Likewise, imagine a situation where you were stressed or scared. You were likely taking shallow, quick breaths. In her book, *The Gifts of Imperfection*, Brene Brown sums this up perfectly, stating "[u]nless we had calm modeled by our parents and grew up practicing it, it's unlikely that it will be our default response to anxious or emotionally volatile situations. For me, breathing is the best place to start. Just taking a breath slows me down and immediately starts to spread calm."[xi] By taking deep, slow breaths, you are modeling for your friend how to achieve their own sense of calm. This has the added benefit of calming you down too. Emotions, whether they are yours or your friends, are stressful and scary! We could all use some calm in our lives and breathing is a great way to get there.

I hope these four simple instructions provide you with a starting point for developing the skill of "holding space" for your friend. Remember, it's not really a natural reaction for most of us. *So, don't get upset if your friend is crying and you forgot to open your hands!* As with all advice, take what works for you and transform it into your own style. Not only will you be rewarded with a skill that is useful in any crisis, your friend will be able to forever access the gift of space that you gave to them in their time of need.

When you can hold space for your friend's grief and your friend can process those emotions, she'll trust your judgment and ability to help her as she navigates her crisis. And from this place, created and maintained by you and your friend, you both can look toward tackling other problems as they arise in the crisis. But more than that, you're now in a position to really listen and help your friend cope with a very important person in their life: their caregiver.

Chapter Three:
Caring For The Caregiver

The simple act of caring is heroic.
~ Edward Albert

The thing about a crisis is that it blossoms beyond the original person, touching all those that come into contact with it. Other than your friend, who else is at the center of this crisis? There is usually a person that bears the daily burden of caregiving — be it physical caregiving (e.g., helping with getting to the bathroom) or the mental caregiving (e.g., dealing with the emotional strain). This person can be a spouse, or a parent, or a sibling. This person can also be a friend or acquaintance or neighbor. Regardless of who is doing the caregiving during your friend's crisis, it is important to understand the complicated relationship that may arise between your friend and their caregiver. As we've discussed in the previous two chapters, there are a surplus of emotions during a crisis that cannot be foisted off for later. As you watch your friend interact with their caregiver, keep in mind that your friend is trying to preserve the relationship roles of the past, amidst terrible change. Helping your friend to manage the difference between their emotions, and the emotions of their caregiver, may be one of the greatest gifts you can give your friend and their caregiver.

Guilt

Before I became sick, my relationship with my husband, Craig, had always been a rather enjoyable dance with each of us alternating who was in the lead. We share a deep love and affection that often translates into a fierce protectiveness of each other. He wants to protect me from harm. I want to protect him from harm. So, frankly speaking, Craig's general role didn't change too much as he stepped into the role as my primary caregiver. He's always been my staunchest supporter. He's always been my personal barometer. Now, though, the care pendulum was swinging far into my court.

As my diagnosis evolved into a full blown crisis, Craig's protector persona became even more pronounced. As such, the delineation between our relationship roles became even more pronounced. Craig was constantly on guard for an emotional break down. And they happened often. He buoyed me, emotionally. He took care of me, physically. He took over when I could no longer function. I became, in some ways, an emotional invalid. As a result, I wasn't able to offer Craig the same amount of support that I would have in any other situation.

From my seat in the eye of the cancer hurricane, I was so thankful that I had such a loving and capable husband. I would not have approached this crisis with any calm or grace if it weren't for his gentle care of me. But that being said, whenever I tried to get a bird's eye view on the crisis and what we were facing, I was wracked with guilt and sadness. I felt like I'd pushed Craig to assume all roles — to include my role as his protector and supporter. I didn't want to give up that role. I wanted to fix things. I didn't want that aspect of our relationship to change in the face of this crisis.

Craig assured me that he was acting out of pure love and not a sense of responsibility. "In sickness and health, Jenny," he would say to me over and over. I still continued to carry this guilt that I wasn't providing a loving atmosphere. I think there was a part of me that didn't believe that I was deserving of his dedication and care and loving. So, sometimes I would shut him out. I would act like all was ok, even when I was torn up inside, because I didn't want to add to his burden. My guilt was getting between Craig and I — between the open communication that we both so desperately needed.

So many friends told me at the time that I "shouldn't feel guilty." I should "just let Craig take care of me." But that didn't acknowledge that the roles Craig and I played in our marriage were changing, and I didn't like the change! We usually shared burdens. I needed to hear that my guilt was ok. That my guilt was natural. I needed to know that my guilt was a sure indication of the depth of my love for Craig. I needed to know that I could release that guilt. I needed to know that releasing the guilt would open the door to deep unconditional love.

When helping your friend manage their guilt, it's a little more complicated than just saying, "It's ok for you to feel the emotions that you have." That's a good place to start, but your friend is looking for a venue to express her guilt, fear, and worry. Just like you did in Chapter Two when she expressed grief, you need to work on holding space for those emotions. Let your friend know that those emotions are neither "right" nor "wrong." Remind your friend, if you told her this before, she only needs to ride this particular emotional roller coaster for 90 seconds before it will come to an end. Not that waiting it out will make the emotion go away, but at the end of that time, the emotion will be less volatile. When things are calmer, your friend can learn to separate themselves from their caregiver. They can learn to acknowledge their guilt and see it for what it is: a failure to accept the situation as it is, right in this moment.

Later in this chapter, I'll give you some specific tools that will help you guide your friend to "stay in her own business," allowing everyone space to manage their own emotions. You can help your friend develop the ability to acknowledge what's happening, feel their own emotions, and separate themselves from the burdens that belong to the caregiver — and the caregiver alone. But until then, let's look at how the changing roles between your friend and her caregiver affect them both.

Changing Roles

Craig was the one that was there when I had to go in for the mammograms and MRIs and blood tests and bone scans and surgeries. He was the one that sat beside me while we waited for the phone to ring. He was the one taking notes each time we went to another doctor, trying to file away the information for us to process later. He made me laugh. He made me smile. He held me in the middle of the night when all I could do was sob. He set me straight when I was angry or sad or upset for all the wrong reasons.

I wanted to be all things for Craig like he was for me. I wanted to provide Craig with emotional support. I wanted to be the person he leaned on and told all his deepest darkest fears. But, I really couldn't be that person, not back then. I could barely take care of my own emotional well-being, how the heck was I going to help anyone else? And Craig wasn't going to add to the mountain of emotions I was dealing with! He wasn't going to "dump in," as we discussed in Chapter One.

Herein lies one of the major issues I have with the principle of the Ring Theory: I believed, and still believe, that I wasn't standing in the middle of those concentric circles on my own. I believe Craig and my girls were standing right there with me. So, I expected us to be able to freely exchange feelings and hurt and pain because, in my opinion, we were at the center of things together. Craig's view of the rings didn't parallel mine, however. Not that he didn't believe he was standing with me in this crisis, but it was as if he was a gatekeeper. He stood guard, protecting the inner circle with all his might.

Craig and I had a particular conversation once, which highlighted our changing roles for me. We were talking about our friends and their support when Craig informed me that Mark (Amy's husband) had not been reaching out to him. I was kind of surprised, even though I knew that, up to that point, their interactions had been reduced to using the instant messenger system attached to the game Words With Friends. Craig told me that Mark's distancing came about not long after he told Mark that his comments and questions weren't helpful. Craig told Mark he didn't need questions, the answers to which had no meaning to either of them; he just needed the occasional "thinking of you" type of interaction. That may seem harsh to some, but it is the kind of direct talk that Craig is known for. So, I suspect that Mark withdrew because he thought Craig needed space. The space wounded Craig, leaving him feeling alone and isolated. Craig called it "ghosting." He told me he was sad because it seemed that the person he considered his closest friend couldn't muster up the courage to be there for him.

Meanwhile, I found out that my friend Tess and her husband, Eddie, had also been trying to navigate the strained contact between Craig and Mark — with Mark. So, here I was trying to fix Craig's hurt. And there they were, trying to fix Mark's hurt. Knowing that Tess and Eddie weren't having much success in changing the situation, either, made me want to be the bearer of Craig's burdens even more acutely. As a result, I spent a lot of time being angry. Angry that Craig was sad. Angry that Mark was not rising to the occasion. Angry that Craig didn't have a good friend to talk to about this. Angry that Mark wouldn't listen to Tess and Eddie.

I so desperately wanted to be in control of something. I wanted to fill this void for Craig. I wanted to make people care for him the way they were caring for me; the way he was caring for me. I wanted him to feel safe and cocooned. I understand, now, that it was impossible for me to fix the situation. I realize that Tess and I made the situation worse, in some ways. No one else could change Mark and Craig's friendship except the two of them. They either had to come together in this crisis or grow apart. And, the burden of deciding how it was going to go down lay squarely on Craig and Mark. What I wanted for Craig was not what Craig wanted for himself. And by trying to push the issue, I just added to Craig's emotional burden.

What I've learned from this is quite simple: everyone is responsible for his or her own emotional wellbeing. As much as I wanted to protect Craig from pain, my role as protector was severely limited in the wake of my cancer diagnosis. And, as much as I wanted to pick the person that would swoop in and fill the position I felt I'd left vacant in Craig's life, it wasn't my person to pick. It was up to Craig. I spent so much time in Craig's business, that I made it my own business — instead of leaving Craig to deal with it as he saw fit.

Remember: your friend is trying to preserve the relationship roles of the past. Notice when your friend is trying to take on the burdens of others. And when you notice that, gently remind your friend that everyone is responsible for their own emotional wellbeing. Remind your friend that there are no positions left "vacant." We are all adjusting to life in the wake of the crisis and doing the very best we can.

Helping Your Friend Stay In Her Own Business

In 2006, thought leader, teacher and author Byron Katie, introduced the idea what there are 3 kinds of business in the universe: mine, yours, and God's.[xii] It's a very short blog post, but the gist of it is that we feel emotional pain when we are not in our own business. Essentially, the pain comes from trying to change things that are beyond your control. Things that are impossible for you to change. This causes stress, worry, and fear. It stops you from being present in the only place where you can effect change: your own life.

Being in God's business means worrying about things that you could never have control over. For me, I was in God's business when I questioned why I got cancer. While there may be all sorts of physical attributes that "contributed to a high risk," at the end of the day, I will never know why I got cancer. These are questions that don't really have good answers. No human has good answers for those questions. Other examples are: "When will I die?" and, "What if my kids get cancer?" Spending time with these thoughts leaves me feeling lost and helpless.

Being in someone else's business is thinking about what others should or shouldn't do. It's trying to effect change by merely stating a preference for something. Examples from the stories I told in this chapter are:

I should not feel guilty.
I am responsible for Craig's happiness.
I must be Craig's protector.
Mark should change how he is acting.

When you're in your own business, you're engaged in caring for the one and only thing you ultimately have any control over in this life: yourself. Following the stories in this chapter, examples of me being in my own business are:

My health is of paramount importance right now.
Craig is responsible for his own happiness.
Craig will protect himself from harm.
Mark is responsible for his own actions.

Here are three clues that your friend is drifting into other people's business:

Statements Using "Should"

The word "should" should be banned from the dictionary. (Other than for use in the sentence "You should not use the word should.") As soon as your friend says anyone "should" or "shouldn't" do something, you'll know they are in someone else's business. The word *should* indicates that a judgment is being made about someone or something. Using my examples from earlier, why should I feel guilty? Craig had already told me that he was acting out of pure love and not responsibility. What did I expect someone who loved me to do? Well, I expect them to take care of me when I'm sick. Which I was and he was. Looking at it from this perspective, it's fairly clear that guilt has no place in that equation.

Similarly, the idea that "Mark should change how he is acting" is avoiding who is responsible for Mark's actions: Mark alone. Tess and I were so far into Mark's business that we couldn't see that we were trying to make a choice for him. We were trying to tell him how to process his own feelings about Craig. And that, frankly, is none of our business.

Statements About Responsibility

This is not as obvious as a "should" statement. But, whenever your friend drifts into talking about what their responsibilities are, keep a close listen. Being responsible for caring for your children isn't being in your children's business. It's a statement of fact: as an adult/parent, you are responsible for your children's wellbeing and welfare. In contrast, being responsible for anyone's *mental* state means you are drifting into someone else's business. I am not responsible for Craig's happiness. I can certainly contribute to it by being a good partner and a loving wife. But at the end of the day, do I get to decide if Craig is happy or not? Nope. He gets to make that decision, himself.

Statements Using "Must"

Unless you're talking about an attorney who has a fiduciary duty to his clients or a doctor who has sworn the Hippocratic oath to protect life, nobody "must" do anything. Pretty much everything we do and say is a choice. So, when I believed "I must be Craig's protector," I was pretty much getting into Craig's business. He didn't need me to be his protector. Heck, he didn't even want me to be his protector. He wanted me to mind my own business and take care of my own health. As soon as I stopped trying to be Craig's protector, I released the emotional burden on myself and on Craig.

When your friend is smack dab in the middle of a crisis within their crisis, it is going to take someone near and dear and close to her (that's *you*, dear friend!) to simply say, "Whose business are you in right now?" And what you need to mean, when you say that, is: "Whose actions or reactions are you trying to control?" It's not always easy to recognize when someone is not in their own business, or to bring yourself to call attention to it. But, by gently directing your friend's attention back to her own business, you are giving her the gift of relief. You are relieving her of the burden of other people's emotional wellbeing. You're giving her the strength and fortitude and power to deal with her own emotions and no one else's. This is a skill that will be important every day for the rest of her life, not just for the duration of this crisis.

When you help your friend stay in her own business, you are empowering her to take care of her own emotional wellbeing. You are giving her permission to put herself first. You're giving her permission to only worry about the things she has the power to change. This simultaneous gift of power and release will never wane. It will last forever. And once you have shown her how to stand in her own business, just as you are standing in your own business, just as the caregiver is standing in their own business, then you all can get along with the business of conquering whatever lays ahead. This important lesson is going to extend into your friend's interactions with everyone in her life, not just her interactions with her caregiver.

Chapter Four:
Helping Your Friend Manage Social Media

Social media is an amazing tool, but it's really the face-to-face interaction that makes a long-term impact.
~ Felicia Day

To summarize so far, three of the greatest gifts you can give your friend during her crisis are: (1) make sure *you* have your own support system, (2) hold space for your friend's emotions and grief with loving kindness, and (3) help your friend to stay in her own business. These three things are very mixed up together, but they all work to help your friend (and importantly, you!) achieve some emotional stability during a time of upheaval. At this point, I hope you're feeling more confident in how to interact with your friend. But what about interacting with the world at large? And what about helping your friend interact with her larger circle of friends and acquaintances?

Social media is a cornerstone of many people's social lives. As such, communication via social media warrants its own special section. If you are like me, a lot of the communication between you and your friend takes place via social media of some type: Facebook, Twitter, Instagram, etc. While the immediacy of social media makes it a great way to stay up to date on a bunch of people at the same time, there are some major pitfalls to this type of communication. Social media and privacy are not easy to balance on a good day. I find that I'm much more apt to share or comment on things on Facebook when, in real life, I would likely not comment at all. When you're in the middle of a crisis, it's even more difficult to manage. The wealth of information can be overwhelming for you and your friend. Messages can be misinterpreted because the context is lacking. Feelings can be hurt when the intention was really just to inform or even spread some cheer. Since you're looking to support and comfort your friend, you need to be quite selective when communicating with your friend on social media.

At the time of my diagnosis, a video was circulating of a woman who was going in for a double mastectomy. In it, the woman and her surgical team dance around to a Beyonce song while in pre-op. The video was showcased on a bunch of major networks and sites: ABC, People Magazine, The Today Show. It got a lot of play. And it got a lot of support from around the world. People were amazed at how confident and joyous and self-assured this woman was, even though she was facing surgery. When I was first exposed to the video, however, I did not feel particularly joyous or happy about it. That video was shared on my Facebook Timeline a mere three days after my own breast cancer diagnosis. As I'm sure you can imagine, I wasn't really in the mood to celebrate the fact that I had cancer. In addition, I still had not told my wider range of friends about my diagnosis. So, when the video, accompanied by the statement, "I'm starting the dance for ya," appeared on my Facebook wall, I freaked out.

Looking back on it now, I can see how the video would be inspiring to people. This woman was joyous in the face of uncertainty. She danced in the face of fear. That's pretty amazing. I also understand why the person that shared it with me would want me to see that video. She hoped to invigorate me. She hoped it would chase away my anxiety. She had no intention of making me uncomfortable or sad or confused. Unfortunately, this video just served to make me feel like I was "doing it all wrong," because I wasn't in the mood the celebrate. Instead, I wasted time trying to decide if I was going to untag myself from the video, checking who had liked it or seen it or commented on it, and wondering what I would do if someone I hadn't told was cued in to my crisis by this simple little post.

All of this anguish was coming on the heels of me telling my close family that I didn't want any news of my diagnosis on Facebook. I'm sure they were surprised, because quite honestly, they know that I spend a ridiculous amount of time on Facebook. I just wasn't ready for another venue where I was going to have to respond to people's inquiries. Of course, I knew that I always had the option of not responding, but that's just not my personality. I would feel guilty if I didn't acknowledge people's posts to me.

Most of my fears didn't come to fruition. The video was "liked" by four people and commented on by two others. Of those folks, only one person wasn't aware of my diagnosis at the time this was posted on my wall. Later, after I shared on Facebook, myself, that I had breast cancer, several people told me they were wondering "what was up with me" because of things they saw on social media. I can only assume this video was one of those things. I was so relieved that these folks did not follow up with inquiries at the time this video was posted. By the time I outed my cancer on Facebook, I was ready to discuss details with a wider audience.

I'll admit though, that for a time after the posting of this video, I was nervous every time I logged onto Facebook. I would do extensive scans of my timeline and news feed for fear of what I was going to find. I knew I was being silly. I knew my friends cared about me and wanted me to know that at all times. But, I couldn't stop the flood of emotion each time I saw something about cancer. I wanted Facebook to be my refuge, the place where I could forget about what was happening with me and get a glimpse at life continuing around me. Instead, I was confronted with some of the following posts on my Facebook Timeline:

> *"I hope it was early detected."*
> *"I hope you're going to supplement with alternative therapies."*
> *"I know you'll be fine."*
> *"Stupid cancer ... Some of us want a new house ... A new car ... A new mobile phone ... To lose weight ... But someone battling cancer wants just one thing, to win the battle. 97% of my friend's won't re-post this, but 3% will. Let's see who does. Please re-post this in honor of someone who lost their battle or for someone fighting it now."*

Obviously the friends that posted stuff like that on my Facebook Timeline just wanted to show me they loved me! They wanted to show some solidarity. They wanted to let me know that they were thinking of me. Instead, the (very sweet) gestures got me dwelling on how much my life sucked. I can't tell you how many times well-intentioned posts like these made me sad or angry or irritated. I was so exhausted from feeling emotions.

To further complicate things, *every* time I got sad, angry or irritated, I *immediately* felt guilt. I knew that my friends, be they close friends or acquaintances, were doing their best to support me and show their love. And they wanted to make sure I was getting the best care imaginable, both physical and mental. So then, my guilt became shame. Shame that I wasn't more thankful. Shame that I couldn't see past my own sadness, anger or irritation, to my friends' true intentions. And shame that I couldn't enjoy the support I was offered.

Simply put, social media complicates matters when someone is in a crisis. Whether it's cancer, a divorce, a sick child, an aging parent - the already amorphous friendship rules change. There are three main categories of people, when it comes to sharing on social media:

- Those who are very comfortable sharing their crisis. There are online sites, such as Caring Bridge[xiii], that are dedicated to allowing people to share their crisis with as wide an audience as they choose. These sites can serve as information repositories and can rally family and friends into a finely tuned support machine. Indeed, every little detail about what's going on, what's happening now, and what's happening next will be on display for friends and acquaintances alike to see and "participate" in.

- Those that share only portions of their crisis. Other people stick to the more broad social media outlets like Facebook and Twitter. You can just share snippets of your life, of your crisis. In fact, people may not even see your posts, but you can still "put it out there." There are, obviously, gradations of sharing on social media sites such as these. People can post extremely long, involved stories on Facebook. Twitter is all about keeping it short.

- Those that will not share on social media. This can include people that don't choose to share information on social media, or people who don't use social media at all.

As a friend who is trying to help someone navigate the terrain of a crisis, you have to keep in mind your friend's preferred method of social media communication. This is a time when it's really important not to focus on how *you* would communicate in a crisis, but rather how your friend would communicate. When in doubt, it is best to assume a conservative approach to sharing on social media when you're talking about what is, really, someone else's business.

When getting ready to navigate your friend's crisis on social media, the question to ask yourself is, simply, has your friend outed their crisis on social media themselves? Your own responses will then vary, depending on the answer to this question.

SCENARIO 1:
Your Friend Has NOT Mentioned Their Crisis On Social Media.

The rule is hard and fast here: you should not make any reference to what your friend is going through on social media. At all.

"But she was so open with me about her issue! Doesn't that mean that I need to show her how much I support her?" Yes. You do. You absolutely need to show support to your friend. She has entrusted you with important information about her life and what's happening with her. But, you should *not* do so on social media! Your options are wide and varied here based on your level of friendship. The next chapter will cover, in detail, some of the best ways I believe you can support your friend other than by holding space. You should channel your love and desire to help into something that will tangibly help your friend. A post on Facebook won't do that. It's too impersonal.

Please note that your friend may or may not be forward enough to tell you, "I don't want this out on Facebook yet." In fact, I would wager to say most people are so busy coping with their feelings and dealing with the day-to-day parts of their crisis, that they don't even think about their "strategy" for telling a wider audience about what they are experiencing. In Chapter Seven, you'll find some strategies to help your friend come up with a communication plan. But, until you know what your friend is comfortable with, as far as communicating to a broader audience is concerned, just follow their lead. Let the type of communication used by your friend be your guide as to how you might (or might not) use social media. More than anything, this will preserve your friend's privacy. If there's been no mention of anything on Facebook, regardless of how they "usually" interact, then you don't get to be the one to mention it. Once (perhaps *if*) your friend decides she is ready for a wider audience, she will do it in her own time and in her own way.

That doesn't mean you can't mention it to your friend, though. If your friend is a "put it all out there" kind of person, but hasn't put anything out there just yet, there is absolutely no harm in asking if she intends to put anything out to the Facebook universe. If and when she is ready to post, then you can apply the principles for scenario 2 or 3 below.

SCENARIO 2:
Your Friend Has Vaguely Mentioned "Things Are Hard Right Now."

This is a tougher situation. Sometimes this type of post is known as "vaguebooking" for obvious reasons. In order to preserve your friend's privacy and to allow them to control the flow of emotion and information, you should let them be the one that outs any details on social media. Although many people interpret "vaguebooking" as a cry for help or begging for attention, realize that your friend is not in their normal frame of mind at this moment. Although your friend has opened herself up to other people asking what's going on with them, they are still controlling the flow of information. They get to decide *who* they tell about their crisis. They also get to decide *how much* they tell someone. There's a big difference between baring your soul to someone — sharing your deepest darkest fears — and telling someone that things are a little in the dump right now.

Before posting anything on social media, there are two questions you should answer:

1. What is my intent in sharing this message?
2. What are the possible ways this message can be received by my friend and others?

First, think about why you want to send a particular message to your friend. Do you want to show him/her you're thinking about them?

Do you just like the message? Do you think that sharing will garner additional support for your friend? Or, do you think that sharing will demonstrate that you're a good friend by acknowledging your intimate involvement with their life? Your intent — or the goal of your communication — is important to discern, because it gives a solid foundation for the communication. The immediateness of social media has seemed to push our society toward communication without thinking it through. When we speak, send or post without purposeful thought behind it, we undermine the gravity of our message. We cheapen the language, somehow, making it more about the "sound" of the communication than the meaning of it. It's almost as if the idea of the communication becomes more important than the content of the communication.

When you have a solid foundation (i.e., reason) for communicating, you can know that you are acting with the best of intentions and love for your friend. If your intent really is just to say, "I'm thinking about you," nothing in the world says that more than just saying the words "I'm thinking about you." If your intent is to share awareness or information with your friend, keep in mind that your friend may not be in a place to properly assimilate that information. By providing that information in a private setting, you allow your friend time to process this information. If your intent is to show others that you know someone well enough to know their secrets, then it may be time to honestly evaluate your own view on friendships and what they entail.

It is equally important to consider how your message might be received by your friend and others. We are quick to respond, but slow to consider the effect of those responses. I have a friend who was very cautious about revealing her cancer diagnosis to anyone. She wasn't comfortable talking about her cancer and, frankly, didn't think that it was anyone else's business. When a relative shaved off her hair in support of this friend, she chose to put a picture of her newly shorn head on my friend's timeline. My friend was appalled. Then, she felt terrible for being appalled. After all, her relative was only trying to show their support! So, then she felt like she had to be all "rah rah" and positive about her relative's solidarity, when really all she wanted to do was run and hide. When she revealed to others that the post upset her, she then had to spend a large amount of time back pedaling, explaining, and even defending her decision to not put her business all over social media. She was exhausted, frustrated, and sad. This is, most certainly, the opposite of what her relative intended when she innocently posted her support publicly.

When you've considered your intentions and how the message might be received by your friend, then you can move forward with a stronger sense of calm. You can act out of the love you're feeling for your friend instead of the fear of "not doing enough" or "not doing the right thing." Now, you're holding space for your friend, as discussed in Chapter Two. You're allowing your friend to deal with her emotions in her own time. You're providing support in a strong, clear manner.

SCENARIO 3:
Your Friend Has Already
"Told The World."

Your friend has told "the world" about what's going on. Sweet. Carte blanche then, right? *Slow down*. This may seem like an easy scenario to navigate. But, frankly, this situation is the most difficult situation for a friend to maneuver through. Why is it harder to navigate when your friend has, essentially, outed themselves? Doesn't that mean that I can "out" my support of them? Yes ... and no. It all comes back to who has the right to share the information. Also, how it's going to make your friend *feel* when he/she gets a good look at how you're demonstrating your support. The *intent* and *receipt* issues discussed in Scenario 2 above still hold true. In fact, they may be even more important in this third scenario, where your friend has fully shared their crisis on social media.

This is confusing territory. It would seem that common sense dictates that once the information about your friend's crisis is "out there," that any message (that is supportive and comes with the right intent) would be an appropriate one. However, I found that I was still quite irritated with particular comments and communications, even when they were in response to my own posts.

It was my pastor who finally convinced me to announce my diagnosis on Facebook. Reverend Mary encouraged me to seek comfort from any avenue that it was available to me. She insisted that Facebook was the modern place to go to receive support, well wishes and, indeed, prayers. Hearing from others in your community (and I don't just mean your physical community, since social media has broadened our sense of community) that they are offering up prayers, well wishes, good thoughts, and positive "ju ju" is an extremely comforting thing. I received such an outpouring of love and support that it staggered me. It is a wonderful thing to behold.

However, there were a few posts that were just tough for me to deal with. Like the one where a friend I hadn't seen in 20+ years lamented all the people she lost to cancer, and then she tagged me in her post. I'm sure her intent was to show me she was thinking about me. And she was scared. And she felt that cancer sucked. But, really all that post did was make me feel like I needed to reassure her that I wasn't going to walk that same road to death. Instead of feeling a sense of peace and support, I was thrust into the role of protector and fear soother. It made me feel like I had to be positive, or I was going to lose this battle for me and for my friend. Remember the reaction I had to Amy's "I can't lose you" statement in Chapter Two? Well, this feeling was pretty much the same.

By far, the power of all the positive comments that I received from people far outweighed those that were bad or misplaced. Reverend Mary was right; Facebook is an amazing place to get support. And what's really cool about it is that all of those comments still lift me up when I'm feeling down. Just going back and reading over all the comments and love in preparation for writing this chapter was enough to put me on cloud nine. So, the lesson to learn here is this: do your best and keep your friend's privacy at the forefront of your thoughts. If you're unsure what to say on social media, stick with posts that aren't about your friend. Then, delve into the next chapter for ways to show your friend that you love her.

Chapter Five:
Showing You Care

The friend who can be silent with us in a moment of despair or confusion, who can stay with us in an hour of grief and bereavement, who can tolerate not knowing...not healing, not curing...that is a friend who cares.
~ Henri Nouwen

Now that we've handled the basics of your grief, your friend's grief, caregivers and social media, you are probably chomping at the bit to get down to the business of helping your friend navigate this crisis. It can be very confusing terrain to traverse, both for you and your friend. You don't want to hurt your friend's feelings. You don't want to cause them pain. But you really *do* want to show them that you care. How do you do that?! The hardest thing, when you don't know what to do or say to someone who is suffering, is figuring out what to do or say. I'll acknowledge that with some people, or some situations, you just can't say or do the right thing. So, before you do anything else, step into your friends shoes again, as we discussed in Chapter One, to put yourself in the right frame of mind to *do* or *speak*.

Just Do

Whenever my friends would offer to do something for me after my diagnosis, it would send me into a spiral of worry: "Am I imposing on them?" "Are they going to be sick of helping me?" "Do they wish they hadn't offered to help?" I'm pretty sure none of my friends ever felt inconvenienced, but I always worried that they did. Although I understand, now, that there is intrinsic reward for my friends in doing things for me, a little ugly voice in my head always made me feel like I wasn't deserving of my friends' help. Although I was woefully bad at accepting help from my friends, I've since learned that the simplest gestures were the ones that meant the most to me. Not that the elaborate ones weren't important. In fact, an elaborate plan put together by a friend was a saving grace for me during a horribly turbulent time for me.

It was really depressing to have a mastectomy in early December. I kept thinking the timing would be great because it's cold outside and everyone is holed up anyway. But it was actually sad. Everyone was out celebrating and I was worrying over how much fluid was collecting in my drains and feeling like they would never be removed. I couldn't help but focus on the fact that the new year was going to start with chemotherapy. I was terrified of chemo. Despite all my protestations and "tough girl" act, I'm sure my friends knew I was balanced on the precipice of extreme fear. I imagine they felt as helpless as I did. They knew I was trying to "stay positive" but also knew I was in for something really big and really unknown. None of my friends, except Tess's sister, had been through what I was facing, so it was new to all of us.

Sometime in mid-December, I opened up my front door to find a gift sitting there. For the next 12 days, my family would open our front door to a surprise gift. Each gift had a type written card with a little rhyme on it that began with, "On the _____ day of Christmas" (where the blank was the day - first, second, third …

you get the idea). The gifts were never delivered at the same time. Sometimes the "drop" was preceded by a knock on the door, sometimes not. We had no idea who was leaving the gifts. But for those 12 days, we didn't really think much about cancer or chemo or radiation or tests. Instead, our minds were consumed with questions about the gifts: Who is responsible? How do they get away without being seen? What is going to be in the next gift? At the end of the 12 days, a bunch of my friends admitted that it was a joint effort: Lana organized it, Carrie did up all the cards, and everyone else chose a day or two to purchase and deliver gifts.

The gifts weren't expensive. They weren't always practical. I'm sure quite a few of them came from the Dollar Store. But it wasn't about the physical gifts. They didn't really matter. What mattered was that when my friends didn't know *what* to do, they did *something* to make me smile. They did something that made my children giggle (and stare out the window, certain that they would catch the person this time). They did something that reminded me of the spirit of the season. They turned a scary time into a time that I will have fond memories of for the rest of my life. It was the most thoughtful, meaningful gift I have ever received. I will never forget the effort and love poured into me and my family over those 12 days.

Although the 12 Days of Christmas was an amazing and elaborate plan that really delivered a tremendous amount of joy, I've since come to understand that doing something simple is just as effective and heartwarming. And *simple* is important when you're at a loss for what to do. Do something that is *easy* for you to do. Do something that's *not* outside of your norm. Whether it's sending a text, writing an e-mail, fixing a meal or coming up with an elaborate 12 Days of Christmas plan, the meaning of these actions is found in the intent behind them. If you're doing stuff to satisfy yourself that you're doing all you can, that intent will show. If you're doing stuff to bring a smile to someone's face, that will show through. If you're doing stuff because you feel guilty, that will also show through. Your friend doesn't want you to do anything for "doing sake" or because you feel bad for them. Your friend wants you to act because you love them. So fill your heart with the love you have for your friend and you will know what to do. I promise.

The things you offer to do for your friend don't have to be things that are out of the ordinary. My friends would probably tell you that they felt the need to do something extraordinary. That they felt like they needed to go out of their way to acknowledge my crisis. But, I'm telling you that extravagance is *not required*! I could write pages and pages about the "not extravagant" things my friends did for me. But, let me just tell you a few of the things people did for me that I found to be the most meaningful. You decide if their actions were extraordinary or not.

My friend Nikki would send me texts at random times of the day (so I know they were spontaneous) when she was thinking of me. Sometimes the texts wouldn't have words, or sometimes there would just be a picture of a really bizarre hairstyle. It sounds so random, but when you're bald and self-conscious, wondering if you're ever going to have hair again, seeing the crazy stuff people do with their hair made me laugh.

My pastor arranged for meals to be delivered from church members. Craig and I were reticent to take this assistance, feeling that others in the congregation must need it more, but we ended up really appreciating it. Not only did the meals mean that dinner was planned for us, they also enabled us to get to know some members of our church better and helped us feel like part of the church community. We ate a lot of roast chicken and homemade mac & cheese. But the repetition of the meals wasn't even an issue. What really mattered was that there were people out there who wanted to make sure we had a good, easy meal in our refrigerator. It felt good to be taken care of.

Other friends delivered meals too. Some dropped off or sent flowers, fruit baskets and balloons. One friend worked at my daughter's preschool for me whenever it was my turn to be the "mommy's helper" in class. A group of friends from law school put together a basket filled with tea, fuzzy socks, and easy to freeze meals. Other friends bought me comfy pajamas, binders to keep all my medical paperwork in, and lotions to soothe my skin.

A set of friends drove my preschool-aged daughter to school every day. I had chemo in the winter, so I had to worry about getting sick, and being in a preschool with snot-nosed, coughing kids wasn't exactly high on the list of "good things to do." Our daughters were in the same class, so they were making the trip anyway. This was, probably, the single biggest piece of help I accepted during my entire treatment. Not only did it give me 30 more minutes in my morning to rest or get stuff accomplished, it kept me out of harm's way.

All of these things helped me physically and mentally. All of these actions showed me I was loved and cared for. All of these actions meant the world to me. But despite all of that, my friends worried that they weren't doing enough. They kept asking what else they could do to help. The problem was, I already felt like I was imposing on them enough! I tried to tell them that everything they offered to me — their time, their love, their patience — was all I truly needed. Now that I can distance myself from it a little bit, I suspect they felt like they weren't doing anything *extraordinary*. And you probably feel like you want to pump it up in the extraordinary department too. But each friend mentioned above? They were definitely doing enough. And you are doing enough just by doing something simple. Sometimes, it's enough for you to just keep doing what you're doing. Most of the time your friend is just so grateful that you've found something that (1) helps them and (2) helps you feel like you're helping. That's all your friend needs.

When You Do Too Much

Once you've found a "thing" to do for your friend, remember that simplicity continues to run the day. Your karmic debt is created by simply loving someone enough to want to do something for them. You don't need to prove to your friend the depths to which you'll go to help them. Ordinary is welcome and just fine. When your life is turned upside down by a crisis, ordinary feels wonderful. Ordinary feels consistent. Ordinary feels life-affirming.

Even though the 12 Days of Christmas was a big deal to me, Amy was a little upset because it hadn't been her idea. "I mean," she said, "I'm your best friend. I'm supposed to be the one organizing gifts and taking care of things for you." At the time, I was so hurt by her statement. I was hurt that she couldn't join me in my happiness because of her own jealousy. I so wanted all my friends to be a team: "Team Jenn," working together while loving on each other and on me and my family. I couldn't understand where she was coming from. Looking back now, though, I understand that the extravagance of the 12 Days of Christmas is what made her the most uncomfortable. It turned on the competitor in her. Amy was so conflicted over what to do and how to help, that she ended up not doing anything at all. Indecision ruled the day. I suspect that she was feeling very sad and a little bit jealous that she wasn't the one that was bringing a smile to my face. She wanted to be the person to do that. Had our roles been reversed, I would have felt very much the same.

Amy's response to the 12 Days of Christmas idea was my first real exposure to the idea that there was going to be jealousy attached to my acceptance of gifts from others. I wish I had known to reassure her that all of the things she was doing for me were enough for me. I wish I had spoken more forcibly when she felt threatened by what others were doing. But, ultimately the problem was that Amy didn't understand that all she had to do was *something simple*. I wish she had known that everything people did, elaborate or simple, brought a smile to my face. Every private message on Facebook, text, phone call, card in the mail, e-mail, and loving note attached to a gift ... they ALL helped me forget myself for awhile. And they meant so much to me that I've kept them all.

One of the absolutely amazing things Amy did for me during my treatment was to be my photographer. Every time I had a major surgery, or I lost my hair, or just had a major outward change, she photographed it for me. She's a wonderful photographer. Exposing your naked body is really vulnerable on the best of days. I felt like my body had betrayed me. I was scared. I was scarred. I felt ugly. I felt embarrassed. And despite all of that, she saw me as I was. No comments. No shock. Just love. She took beautiful pictures to document my physical journey. But it's more than that. You can see the psychological journey in those photos, too. I have no idea what I'm going to do with those photos. Maybe nothing. Maybe I'll show them to my daughters someday. I don't know. But that picture taking meant so much to me. It helped me see my progress over time. It helped me feel beautiful in my own skin again. That is an unparalleled gift. But in the wake of that unparalleled gift, Amy felt like she wasn't doing enough for me. The idea that she thought so lowly of the gift she was giving me makes my heart ache. I wish she'd known that what she was doing was enough. I wish she'd known that it wasn't a competition. I wish she'd known I wouldn't measure the gifts — that I have a heart big enough for them all.

Remember the story of Carrie in Chapter One? Carrie was the one who set up the "Neighborhood Cares" website? You might be thinking, at this point, "Why was that the wrong thing to do?" It's a little counterintuitive — but bear with me. The answer is this: it wasn't simple enough. Carrie was trying to do too much at a time when I needed people to do less. Right after my diagnosis, I couldn't quite grasp what all of this cancer stuff was going to entail. The calendar felt like a long, involved, elaborate plan for my care. Now, I understand that it was just a way to organize people that wanted to help. *I get that.* But at the time, it just seemed so huge and so inclusive and so over the top. We didn't even know how I was going to respond to treatment yet! If I was going to be throwing up from chemo, the last thing I wanted was someone knocking at the door, let alone with food I couldn't eat. Had Carrie kept with her simple gestures, like hugging me every time we saw each other, that would've been just fine.

So, don't go into this crisis thinking you can't do anything for your friend. Don't go into this crisis thinking that your friend will be better off without you. Don't go into this crisis planning to be the best gift-giving-texting-driving-to-appointments-chef your friend has ever seen. Just stop. Stop beating yourself up. Stop competing with yourself. Stop competing with her other friends, many of whom are your friends. The last thing your friend needs is for you to keel over from exhaustion and worry about whether or not you are pleasing her. It is never pleasing to know that people are stressed about doing something for you! It is infinitely pleasing, however, to know that people care. Do what comes easiest to you, whether that's reaching out on e-mail or driving or taking photos. Every action counts. And every action will bring you closer to your friend and she to you.

Just Say

When a friend is sick, silence surely is not golden. I was most hurt by the people who I expected to comfort me, yet I didn't hear from them. Looking back, I realize that some of the blame lies with me. I didn't contact all the people that I thought would contact me. So, how were they to even know that I was in a crisis, if I didn't tell them? And when I did reach out, I asked people to respect my privacy. But then I wondered why they didn't tell others about it. I was, unknowingly, creating a double standard for my friends. Talk about me ... but only within the rules that I haven't laid out for you. Those are tough expectations to meet. I was such a mess.

I had been volunteering with the Ulman Cancer Fund for Young Adults for five years before I was diagnosed with breast cancer. The day after my diagnosis, I had an immediate support group. People who knew me and whom I knew. People who'd been where I was going.

People I could ask about doctors and treatments. I felt so much relief knowing there were others out there who had walked this path before me. That "alone" feeling that a scary diagnosis can leave you with? It was gone when I realized just how deep my support system was. I think I really expected all the people tied to this organization, both cancer survivors and other volunteers, to be the people who could empathize with my plight the most. They saw cancer regularly. They talked about it more openly than most. So, I was really surprised when several people that I felt pretty close to didn't reach out to me, at all. I don't know exactly what I expected, but my experience did not meet my expectations.

This was the first of many such lessons for me. The main lesson being: speak up. Speak up when you want people to know stuff. If you don't, how can you expect them to know it? This same lesson applies to you as you watch your friend navigate their crisis. How can your friend know you care if you don't say anything? You don't have to write a 100 page paper to tell someone you're sorry things are tough right now. You don't have to wait until you see them in person now that we have things like text, e-mail, snail mail, and social media. Reach out. You will be glad that you did and your friend will be so grateful. Remember how I've kept every communication people sent me when I was sick? All the e-mails, notes, cards, etc.? Well, I don't just still have them. I still read them. I treasure them. Whenever I am feeling down, I have an immediate stash of proof that I am loved and not alone. You can give your friend no greater gift.

For those times when you're not quire sure what to say to your friend, I've compiled examples of the messages that made me feel the most cared for and loved and put them into an easy, accessible format. You can find this **free** resource online at jennmcrobbie.com.

Before you go off and get lost to the Internet, however, I want you to know that the messages that really made me feel extra loved and extra cared for said something to the effect of: "Thinking about you. No need to respond, just wanted you to know that I love you."

Why is this a key sentiment? Because it tells your friend that you're not expecting a back and forth exchange. It tells your friend that your sentiment requires no feedback. It shows your friend that you understand that its hard to acknowledge people's love for her. Mostly, though, it shows your love plainly and simply without need of anything elaborate to back it up.

When You Say Too Much

I was amazed at the stuff people would say to me after I told them I had cancer. The responses ranged from "that sucks," to full dissertations on what I should be doing to "take care of myself." I resented the implication that I had cancer because I, obviously, hadn't been taking care of myself. I resented the comments that I had "the good kind of cancer." I stressed every time someone asked me, "Do you know what caused it?" Or, every time someone told me about someone else's cancer journey, I felt a little less important and more than a little silly for feeling overwhelmed and frightened.

I know that every single comment came from the heart. I refuse to believe otherwise. Every person that I communicated with was looking at the fear in my face. They saw how precious life was. They saw the indiscriminate nature of illness. And when you're confronted by that kind of thinking, you'll often develop a condition that I lovingly call verbal diarrhea. It's when you just can't stop talking. You know you need to "Just Say" as we discussed above, but your common sense has somehow left you. When it happens to me, I'm often horrified at the things that are coming out of my mouth. I can't believe that my internal filter is just off.

This is going to happen to you at some point in your life, if it hasn't happened already. And it may happen at some point during your friend's crisis. You might just be thinking aloud. You might just have forgotten who you were talking to. You might just be trying to fill the silence. When this happens … own the moment. Laugh. Change the subject. Or acknowledge it and tell your friend you're sorry. Be honest. Your friend understands because this has, and will happen to her again, too.

One of the things that's really hard to explain to people when you're a breast cancer survivor is that the crisis … the cancer … the sickness … it's not about breasts. Of course, it happened or is happening *to* your breasts, but it's more about the fact that your body has produced something that might kill you. You certainly think about losing your breasts or that your body image is going to change because of surgeries to your breasts. But at the end of the day, this is about *cancer* — heck, my *life* — *not* about boobs. Stated more broadly, this is about the crisis itself, nothing less.

Nevertheless, I can't tell you the number of jokes made — by friends, and even by me — about how lucky I'd be to "get bigger boobs" or about how my husband must be so excited because now I'll have "perky boobs" back. I'll admit that I probably perpetuated the problem by telling people that my insurance company gifted me new boobs and a tummy tuck for my 40th birthday. In the wake of such a major illness, though, a little humor can go a long way. Laughter really is the best medicine. That being said, joking can come at a price. A joke is funny when it's told the first time and in the right context. It begins to lose its allure by the 100th time you've heard it. No matter what the joke was, or who was laughing when it was first told.

Arthur is the kind of person who jokes a lot. He loves to pick on people. And most of the time, its pretty endearing. He and I have an interesting rapport — a back and forth that results in a tremendous amount of laughter. We are sarcastic. It works for us...mostly. The conversation started out like any other, when he jokingly said I was lucky that I was going to be able to get some work done on my breasts. I laughed. I agreed. I even talked about how they were going to be back where they were when I was 20, instead of where they sat now. But the conversation didn't end there. I don't remember the exact words, but the gist, as I recall it: "Don't you want to have bigger boobs," "Craig will be happier if you have bigger boobs," "Have you considered a double mastectomy so that they are both perfect?" I felt a lump form in my throat. He just couldn't stop himself. I felt trapped.

After listening for awhile, maybe too long, I finally said, "Arthur, I don't want to talk about this any more. I'm done. If you bring it up again, I will punch you in the face." I will never forget the look he gave me. He was appalled. He was sorry. He was uncomfortable. He was sad. He realized, at that moment, that the verbal diarrhea had gotten the best of him. And he felt terrible. What's worse is, I felt terrible too. I was fighting back tears. Definitely not the way we envisioned the conversation going when we first started it.

For me, joking is often a coping mechanism for when I am uncomfortable. So, the people around me joked a lot during my treatment. Remember the texts from Nikki with the funny hairstyles? That was a way for us to bond and to bring some light heartedness to a pretty crappy situation. And I appreciated it. All of it. The laughter definitely lifted the burden of sadness that I carried with me everywhere. That being said, direct jokes about your friend's crisis are best left to the person in the crisis. Please understand that, often, when your friend jokes about their crisis, it's really just a means for your friend to open up discussion about what they're thinking about. It's a way to relieve the stress they are feeling about their situation. It's not really an open door for you to begin ripping on your friend, or coming up with reasons why their crisis is going to be "SO AWESOME" in the end.

It's hard to know when a joke has gone too far. But most of us can, in hindsight, pinpoint when a conversation started going downhill. How do you short circuit that before you end up crumpled at the bottom of the hill with your foot in your mouth? You rely on your intuition.

You're thinking...*My intuition?! EGADS! I don't have intuition, lady!* Well, sure you do. You're just not attuned to listening to it. In Martha Beck's book, *Steering By Starlight*, she discusses something called the "Shackles Test." Martha uses the Shackles Test to help clients tell the difference between instinctive fear and the fear you feel when taking a calculated risk. An instinctive fear is the type of fear you feel when walking down a street alone at night. The fear you feel when you're asking your boss for a raise, however, is the fear you feel when taking a calculated risk. Oddly, your feeling state when doing each of those things is quite similar. Start by asking yourself: *Does this serve my destiny?* Meanwhile, gauge your body's physical reaction, and you can determine if you're experiencing an instinctive fear, or fear associated with taking a calculated risk.[xiv]

Imagine what it feels like to be walking down the street at night alone. In the distance, you see hooded figures blocking your path. Your instinct is probably telling you to run away to protect you from this potentially dangerous situation. In response, your body likely reacts. Sweaty palms. Upset stomach. Unbidden tears. Ask yourself, *How does this serve my destiny?* Not very well, right? Walking down that street is bad. These are the feelings you have when experiencing an instinctive fear. These are the types of feelings you get when you feel "shackled." When you feel shackled, you should avoid that situation.

Now, imagine how you feel when you're getting ready to ask your boss for a raise. You probably have some of the same physical reactions: sweaty palms, upset stomach, maybe even tears. But then ask yourself: *Does this serve my destiny*? Or, *Do I deserve this raise?* Chances are, you feel differently, don't you? You don't feel shackled. Rather, those chains fall to the ground, setting you free. It's still scary to go ask, but how do you feel about the outcome of this risk? Airy, light, carefree? This is shackles off sensation. When the shackles are off, you should feel free to jump into that fear you're feeling.

I believe you can use a variation of the Shackles Test to determine if you've said (or are saying) too much. This time, I want you to ask yourself: *Am I serving the conversation?* This twist can help guide you in conversations with your friend. I'm willing to bet that if Arthur had tuned into his body — or observed mine — he would've have felt the tension rising. As he continued to joke, his palms might have started sweating. His mind might have started racing, looking for ways to stop talking. He might have seen me stop making eye contact, or shifting my feet. Upon reflection, Arthur would have been feeling "shackling" feelings. Had he known that, he could have stopped and changed the subject right then and there.

Throughout this crisis, you're going to say some funny stuff, whether you intend to or not. You and your friend are going to laugh about it. It will lift their sadness, as you've intended. Just don't beat that horse long after it's dead. Observe your friend. Savor that moment of light heartedness with your friend. Love the way they look when they laugh. Enjoy being the cause of a lingering smile on their face. Notice when they begin to wring their hands. Notice when they cross their arms across their chest. When you see these cues, don't push it. Don't keep on until you've stuck your foot in your mouth, because then you and your friend will be swimming upstream instead of going with the flow of the moment.

Once your intuition is attuned and you sense yourself going down that rabbit hole, how do you stop? The answer is simple. Which, of course, means that it's easy to for me to put on the page, but harder to put into practice. I alluded to it above. When you're caught in a spiral of saying things you can't believe you're saying out loud:

Change the subject.

Seriously. It's that simple. Make a 90 degree turn in your conversation. Stop short. Pinch yourself. Whatever you can do to stop the words in your mind from coming out of your mouth, do it. Your friend will understand, because she's been in that position before. We all have. You don't even have to end the joke gracefully. Just let it go by ending the discussion. Finis. Done.

There is something else you can do, but it's infinitely more difficult to put into practice for the vast majority of us humans. Changing the subject is perfectly fine, and will work in most situations. So, it's a solid reaction once you realize your foot is moving toward your mouth. But if you're really bold and brave, then your best move is to own up to what you've said. That entails facing the error head on. You'll say something like, "I'm so sorry. I just noticed that you're looking at me like you want to punch me in my face. And, I probably deserve it. Please forgive me. Let's move on and talk about more mundane things." The difference between this method and the "change the subject" method is the ownership of it all. You have to admit that you've done something wrong. And that's not easy to do. Or, you may not feel like you've done something wrong, so why should you apologize for being yourself?

The key is understanding that you're apologizing for *causing* discomfort to your friend — not necessarily for *what* you said or *how* you said it. You probably meant, in the best way possible, what you said. But, you didn't foresee your friend's reaction, and that's worth apologizing for. Once you're doing and saying and handling your friend's crisis like the amazing friend you are, you're going to be feeling much better about the prognosis. You're going to be feeling better about your friendship. You're going to be feeling like you and your friend can handle any situation that arises, and you might be right. Or you might not. In the next chapter we'll talk about when you think you know better than your friend, and how you sometimes do, and you sometimes don't.

Chapter Six:
Giving Good Advice

It is important to our friends to believe that we are unreservedly frank with them, and important to friendship that we are not.

~ Mignon McLaughlin

It seems like such a simple thing. When you see your friend suffering, or feeling left out, you want to help. You want to tell them how to be included. You want to tell them how you've succeeded in this arena. You want to hold their hand while they walk through the fire. You want to fix it. I can't tell you how many times I've found myself spouting out advice to the people around me — especially my friends — when they haven't asked for it. It's in my nature. When I catch myself telling people what to do, I cringe inside: *Ugh. Here I go again.* But I can't always stop myself. I *so* want to help.

This is most evident, now, when people come to me with questions about breast cancer. I'll start spouting off next steps, how to move your body to avoid tightness, how to eat, how to interpret pathology reports — from the simple, to the not-so-simple. And at the end of these conversations, I always feel so much better about myself. I've spread the love, you know? I've shared my experience and that's what makes experiences worth having, right? Except…

When I really step back and look at these interactions with a discerning eye, I realize that I have not always had the best reaction when the shoe is on the other foot. In my experience, there are two types of advice. It'll either be advice regarding "doing it all wrong" or advice regarding "doing it all right." Offering either type of advice comes with pitfalls, but you can remedy either situation in the same manner.

"You're Doing It All Wrong"

It was a big deal for me when I finally put my diagnosis on Facebook. I understood that putting myself out there meant that I was opening myself up to lots of suggestions and advice from other people. But, I felt prepared. I told you in Chapter Four that my pastor convinced me to use Facebook as a base of support. And she was right. It was a wonderful support for me. But, still, I wasn't prepared for my own reaction when I received the unsolicited message that I was going about my cancer treatments all wrong.

The day I announced that I had breast cancer on Facebook was the day my hair began to fall out due to chemotherapy. When I couldn't stand any more handfuls of hair in my wastebasket, I had Craig take it all off. Then, I put on a smile and posted a picture of my bald self on Facebook, explaining the situation. The responses poured in. They were so supportive. Some shock. Some surprise. It was a little overwhelming. But in a good way. I was feeling pretty happy because every time I checked back into Facebook, another positive comment appeared. That feeling ended when I got the following comment: "…hope you also supplement with alternative therapies for cancer. If I see anything particular I will send it your way. I had previously researched some theories…"

WHAT?! My reaction was pretty instantaneous. And pretty visceral. Don't get me wrong, I can look back now and completely understand that this woman's suggestion was meant to help me. She wanted me to know that there were other alternatives out there. She wanted to make sure that I was taking care of myself in the most well-rounded way possible. But at the time, I couldn't fathom was how she had gleaned, from my one Facebook post, that I was looking for advice. And the phrasing implied that I should be open to the idea of alternative therapies or … or what? I had no idea. To even suggest that I could be doing more or should be doing more, even when accompanied by an offer to "do the research for me," was presumptuous. I was hurt and confused by the idea that my choices, whatever they might be, would be incomplete if I didn't include her ideas.

Thus began my experience with people that, although they meant well, suggested that I was doing it all wrong. The hardest part of receiving unsolicited advice is when it isn't even framed as advice. Instead, it's framed as a general statement: "I hope you caught it early." Or, it's framed as experience: "My mother didn't have to wait so long for *her* test results." There's also the outright questioning of my choices: "Why in the world would you get a unilateral mastectomy over a bilateral mastectomy?" Most of the time, though, the advice came in the form of an innocuous suggestion, like when people would invite me to places because they were sure I "needed to get out of the house."

All of these questions or comments may seem reasonable to you. You want to help. You want to share your knowledge with your friend. What makes the "You're Doing It All Wrong" approach so hard to spot, is that you don't even know or feel like that's what you're telling your friend. You're just offering suggestions because you want to see them thrive in the face of adversity. If you're thinking that perhaps I was a little too sensitive, I ask you to look beyond the intent of the messages I received from friends.

I think we can all agree that the intent behind these statements
(and really, most things people say)
*is **not** to hurt.*

But just because a statement isn't *meant* to hurt, doesn't meant that actual hurt isn't *caused*. Let me show you what I mean using the statements above.

I'm sure that the friend hoping that I "caught it early" intended to reassure me that my cancer was curable. But the result of that statement was me wringing my hands over the fact that my cancer WASN'T caught early. I spent a crazy amount of time trying to figure out what I could have done to "catch it earlier." I fretted over the fact that I hadn't done all I could have done. I cried thinking that it was my fault my cancer had progressed to Stage 3A. It took my doctors and several classes on breast cancer to convince me that even if I had "caught it earlier," nothing would have changed. My treatment would probably have been the same. So, this simple statement caused me months of pain and heartache. Surely, *not* the intent, but harm was caused anyway.

In the instance of wondering why it was taking so long for my test results to come back, and questioning my choice of mastectomy, I'm sure my friends intended to galvanize me to advocate on my own behalf. But the result of those statements was to leave me wondering why my friends couldn't trust my judgment, or the judgment of the team I'd put together to help me beat this cancer.

And the people that were sure I needed to leave the house intended to get me back to living life. But the result of those statements was to make me feel like I was a failure when I didn't want to leave the house. I questioned myself and berated myself when I was embarrassed to show my bald head to the world.

Remember the techniques in Chapter Three? When you taught your friend that staying in her own business would empower both her and her caregiver? You taught your friend that it would give room, for both your friend and their caregiver, to get things done and to love each other in the process. Well, now I'm going to be *your* friend. And I'm going to say to you, very gently:

"Who's business are you in when you're giving your friend advice on how they should cope with their crisis?"

Honestly, answer that question. Are you standing firmly in your own shoes and extending a hand to your friend who's fallen?

Or are you stepping into your friend's shoes and trying to stand up for them? In the latter, you've wrested control from your friend. You've taken over the situation. It might not seem that way, but by imposing your own idea of how your friend should cope with her crisis, you are leaving her very little room to do things her own way. She'll be jumping through the hoops you've created, answering your questions, satisfying your expectations instead of dealing with things her own way. And at the end of the day, the only way your friend can "do" this crisis, and make it through intact, is in her own way.

In each example above, the commenter was most certainly "in" my business. She was diving deep into my choices for my treatment, and how I was choosing to handle my crisis. While she was rooting around in my business, I wasted precious energy and thought putting myself into her business, in order to analyze why I was doing it so wrong. So, we were each in each other's business instead of our own, and nothing could get done that way. She couldn't help me, because I didn't know what I needed help with. And I couldn't help me, because I didn't know what I needed help with. We were at a stand still.

I understand that all the unsolicited advice I was offered came from a place of love. From a place of wanting to help. From a place of not wanting me to suffer needlessly. And if you are thinking of offering some advice to your friend right now, realize that there *is* a way to offer advice that is *not* getting into your friend's business:

Choose I statements over YOU statements.

Here's an easy example of an I statement versus a YOU statement:

"YOU" STATEMENT: "…I hope you also supplement with alternative therapies for cancer. If I see anything particular I will send your way. I had previously researched some theories for my aunt."

"I" STATEMENT: "…I know a lot about alternative therapies for cancer because I researched them for my aunt. If you're ever interested in hearing about them, I'd be happy to share all the information with you."

I know what you're thinking: "The first example used the word I!!" And "that second example used the word "you!!" How is either a "you" or an "I" statement?" You grammarians would be technically correct. But, I ask you to look at the primary focus of each statement. With the "You" statement, it's all about what the commenter wants me to do. She even goes so far as to offer to help me do it. But keep in mind, I haven't asked for this advice. So, it's placing me in the position of feeling like I've done it all wrong. This is disempowering.

In contrast, the "I" statement is all about the commenter. It's about her own experience. It puts me in the driver's seat regarding alternative therapies. I can follow up on my own, knowing she's a resource. I can take her up on her offer of help. I can ignore her statement. Either way, I am the one that is making the decisions about my own crisis. This is empowering.

This can be a real change in your style of communicating, and it can take quite a bit of work. To give you a head start on trying this simple shift in language, I've created a **free** resource with more examples of You statements vs. I statements. You can find this resource, plus many more here: jennmcrobbie.com.

Even if you make this shift in communication style, you may notice that your friend is taking some people's advice, and not others. I was so very lucky that I had volunteered with an organization that helped young adult cancer survivors long before my own diagnosis. As soon as I was diagnosed, I was surrounded by a community of people who "got it." I would call up these friends for comfort, or to talk about things ranging from which doctor to pick to how to handle other people's reactions to my news. Amy never said it, but I could tell that she was sad that I wasn't turning to her for solace or advice. The thing is, these people had walked the road that I was embarking on. They knew this journey. And I needed that information, both for its pure factual power, and for the emotional support it offered me. If other people had survived this road, it meant I would, too. I never spoke to Amy about her feelings, but I always felt a little bad when I realized I called one of my "new" friends over her.

If you're in the "she's not taking my advice" camp, your feelings may be pretty hurt right about now. Especially if the people your friend is taking advice from haven't been part of her life for as long as you have. You might even feel a little betrayed. Please know that often your friend will take advice from others whose business looks a lot like hers at the time. If she is turning to new people who have had similar experiences, she isn't choosing their friendships over yours. Your business just may not mirror hers at the time. But, that does not mean that you are not a useful part of your friend's support team. You are. And you remain a useful part as long as you stay in your own business, and keep your friend in his or her own business.

"You're Doing It All Right"

At the same time I was diagnosed, another mom, whose son attended my daughter's school, was also diagnosed with cancer. Julie's cancer was much more aggressive than mine, so her treatment regimen was considerably different. Where my chemo treatments lasted for about 3 hours, hers lasted for 8 hours. Where I had surgery to remove the cancer before anything else, she had radiation and chemo beforehand, in order to shrink her tumor to the point where it could be operable. Yes, we both had "cancer," but there weren't a lot of similarities in our treatment or even prognosis.

I saw Rick, Julie's husband, on a fairly regular basis. Any time I saw him, he'd corner me. He'd tell me how great I looked, and how he couldn't believe how much energy I had. He was always gushing with compliments. I'll be honest, it made me uncomfortable. It was hard to accept compliments when I was in the throes of treatment. I didn't feel like I was doing anything special. I was just going about my journey in the only way I knew how.

Invariably, he'd end up telling me that Julie was definitely not as upbeat as I was. He would compare the two of us: I was more energetic, she slept all the time. I picked up my daughter from school, she could barely leave the house. I smiled when I saw people, she was grumpy. He would then try to set up meetings between me and Julie: "Maybe if you talk to her then she'll be more upbeat like you. She's just not as positive as you are. Give her your tips to be more positive and have more energy."

Of course I engaged in platitudes, "Oh, I'm sure she's doing great." I politely bowed out of these meetings. But, I felt terrible every time I said no, or skirted the situation, or avoided Rick. If I was doing so much better than her, shouldn't

I be helping her? Was I being selfish by not visiting? I didn't know her very well, but shouldn't I be offering my tips? Shouldn't I be concerned about another human, another woman, who was suffering?

Since I'm a life coach, a lot of people assume that I'm perpetually ready to provide deep and meaningful help to anyone that crosses my path. While that might be close to the truth on a good day, when I was in the middle of treatment I could barely cope with my own day-to-day experiences. I didn't have the capacity to focus on how someone else was coping with their own treatments for a totally different type of cancer. Don't get me wrong: I asked Rick for updates and I was (and am) genuinely concerned for Julie's welfare. But if I spent all my time focusing on what other people were going through at the time, well, *then* whose business would I be in?

Rick rested on his own affirmations that I was a "warrior" and a "fighter" and "doing so well." Even when I tried to tell him how I was actually doing, all he really heard was that I was doing better than his wife. These conversations served to cage me rather than bring me comfort.

He had no idea how I was coping with my cancer treatments. He saw me on the days I was willing to share myself with "the world." The days when I didn't feel like a cancer patient. He didn't see me on the days when I bawled for hours or did nothing but complain. He didn't see me on the days that I believed I was weak. He didn't see me on the days that I lacked hope. And so, his compliments? They made me feel like a fraud. How could I live up to his glowing expectations? And to make matters worse, his flawed perception that I was "doing it all right" ended up driving him to ask me to get involved in he and his wife's business. He was trying to draw me in, to get me to tell him what to do, and how to do it. The problem with that is two fold: (1) I'm not Julie, so our experiences could never be the same, and (2) it threatens to pull me out of my own business and into their business.

In short, Rick was mistaking my business for Julie's business. He wanted Julie's business to resemble mine, so he wanted me to help him change her. And that's not helpful to anyone in a crisis. Obviously, he had the best of intent with regard to his compliments to me and what he wanted for his wife. But by telling me that I was "doing it right," he was turning my experience into a one-dimensional experience. This short-sighted view of my crisis — or anyone's crisis — doesn't serve reality.

When someone offers me a compliment, it's like taking a snap shot in time. "You look really nice today," freezes that moment in time for me. My brain files that away under "awesome things that happened today." Rick's compliments to me, however, weren't capturing a moment in time. They were encapsulating my entire experience and smooshing them all into one neat little manual entitled, "How to Do Cancer The Right Way." The problem with this is not that Rick admired how I was walking my journey. Not at all. The problem was that it failed to acknowledge that these interactions did not comprise my whole experience. My whole experience, in his mind, was encapsulated by positivity and warrior spirit. And he desperately wanted that for his wife, which is admirable and lovable.

I'm not saying that you shouldn't compliment your friend on how they are handling their crisis. But, I am asking that you consider that anything you observe is a snapshot in their day. In their lifetime. In this moment of the crisis. Offering up positivity to a friend is always warranted. But, also acknowledge that your friend doesn't have to "do it all right." After all, there is no one way to do anything. So, there isn't really a "right" way to do anything. There's just your friend's way. So, a compliment *does* go a long way. But, it doesn't cover the entire distance.

When you're able to take a step back from advising or complimenting your friend, you can get fully into your own business. From there, you can help your friend navigate their crisis from their space, in their own business. Remember, in the beginning of this chapter, how I told you I can be a breast cancer know-it-all? When I really practice the tips in this chapter, I realize that it's much better for me to just be present with my friend and let her guide the conversation. It's so much better to answer her questions and let her arrive at her own conclusions, than to fill her mind with what worked for me.

I won't always get this right. And neither will you. It's a constant battle between our desire to help and our desire to be right. But we'll get it when we can step back from being right, just for a moment. The hidden gift is to allow your friend to have her own experiences. This will be empowering and rewarding. This is the depth of support we can all benefit from, crisis or not.

Even if you stay in your own business, and your friend stays in her business, you might find that your friend isn't responding or communicating with you. When this happens, it might be time to examine the intersection of your business a little more closely.

Chapter Seven:
Breaking Down
Communication Barriers

The language of friendship is not words but meanings.
~ Henry Mark Thoreau

You know those extra long receiving lines people do at weddings? Where you're walking into the reception and you have to shake hands with everyone from the ring bearer to the father of the groom (whom you wouldn't know from Adam except he's in a tux and standing next to the groom)? It's certainly a little awkward for the guests, but they're usually pretty excited because they get to see the bride and groom up close. That makes all the ancillary hand shaking a lot less troublesome. When you're *in* the wedding party though, and the line slows because someone is telling the bride their life story, I find that so incredibly awkward. I never quite know what to say to the person standing in front of me with their hand outstretched. And it's in those moments when the verbal diarrhea I talked about in Chapter Five hits me the hardest. Things just start spilling out of my mouth. I have since learned to curb this inclination by falling silent. My mantra: "smile, handshake and avoid prolonged eye contact at all costs!"

I felt this same sense of dread when it came to disseminating information after I found out something new about my diagnosis or treatment. I didn't quite know what to tell people. I wanted to just spill my guts, but I always worried that would make people feel uncomfortable around me. It didn't feel right to censor the information altogether, either. I never quite knew how people would respond to what I'd just learned about my illness. So, like in the receiving line, I tended to offer a smile, a handshake and I avoided eye contact at all costs.

This was fine for some people, mostly my acquaintances who weren't overly invested in the details. They just wanted to know that I was okay, and they could observe that with their own eyes. Perfect. My close friends and family, however, wanted to know the nitty gritty. They wanted to know every detail. My mother-in-law was a nurse, so she was able to balance being compassionate while focusing on the medical details. Talking to my own mother, however, was hard for me, because she couldn't hide the pain in her face when she was forced to think about what her baby was going to endure. It was an awkward dance, but we navigated it as best we could. And we all got better at it as time went on.

Craig took on the major role of communicating the "details" to everyone. We put together an e-mail list with everyone on it right before I had my mastectomy. Craig used that list to tell people stuff as it came up. It was great, because I didn't really have to do anything to communicate with folks. Sometimes I would read the responses from folks, and sometimes Craig would read them to me.

Our organizational planning ended after that, though. The overwhelming nature of treatment and surviving just got in the way. As a result, communications with people were sporadic and sometimes strained. Looking back, I wish I had been more specific with Craig regarding the long-term plan for letting everyone know what was happening. Without that, it became a difficult part of the process.

If your friend seems to be languishing in the communication department, there are a few things you can do to help. Before I tell you those things, though, it is extremely important that you make sure you're not stepping on the caregiver's toes. If the caregiver is overloaded with the other duties, then helping with or taking over the communication with others would be an amazing asset for your friend and her caregiver. I'll be honest: in my situation, allowing a friend to be responsible for communication would *not* have worked. This was one of the things that Craig wanted to do. In fact, I had assigned communicating with the broader group to him. We would plan together. This was a bonding time for us. He would have been offended if someone had waltzed in and tried to take this duty off of his plate.

So, knowing that, your first task is to make sure that this is a duty that even *needs* to be picked up by someone else! If so, have at it … full steam ahead! If not, then there is nothing lost at all by offering your assistance. Maybe you can take over one aspect of the communication (e.g., letting your friend's office know what's happening) to lighten the burden. Or, maybe your simple act of asking if you can help can let your friend and their caregiver know that you feel out of the loop. Either way, a possible way to prevent a breakdown in communication is to help your friend build their communication plan.

Build A Communication Plan

It's a difficult line to walk, as a friend. You don't want to be hounding your friend during her crisis; but you also don't want to be on the outskirts or get left behind. The thing is, we should always be in open communication with our friends, crisis or not. Honest, heartfelt assurances that we are loved are, to me, what keeps a friendship going. A crisis often thrusts people into positions they may not be ready for. It can be an opportunity to raise the level of your friendship. It can be an opportunity to raise the level of communication. It can be an opportunity to raise your friend out of the darkness of her crisis, and into the light of friendship. It *can* be, but it doesn't always work out that way.

You're probably thinking to yourself that this is a lot of pressure on you. And I'm not going to lie, it might be. Particularly so, if communicating is not your strong point. But, who are we, as people, if we don't communicate with each other? How can our relationships deepen if we are not communicating with each other? Being a friend isn't always easy, I'm afraid. In fact, it can be a lot of work. But you're here and reading this … so you're up to the task. The relationships that are a lot of work are the ones that are worth fighting for.

Knowing what I know now, I wish I had a friend who would sit down with me and make a communication plan. If that sounds so *not* touchy-feely, that's because, well, it's not. It *is* a perfect way to tap into your friend's emotions in a rather safe setting. You want to help your friend through this difficult time, and maybe creating a communication plan doesn't sound as helpful as cooking a meal or taking care of the kids, but believe me, it can be one of the greatest gifts you give. This is a time you get to ask your friend what feels good *to her*. It's a time you get to give your friend permission to tell you (and potentially others) exactly what she wants and is looking for going forward. It's a time you get to help your friend verbalize her boundaries, instead of hiding behind her emotions in shame. Can you see what a gift that is? Can you see how this would bring your friendship closer?

The practicalities of setting up a communication plan will likely differ depending on your friend and depending on her crisis. But, that being said, the steps are pretty standard. When preparing the plan, you can follow the 5 W's and 1 H:

WHO does your friend need to communicate with? This is purely list making. You can start with listing all the people your friend is acquainted with or, alternatively, all the people that are aware of your friend's crisis. You can divide people into categories based on their relationship to your friend. Family. Co-workers. Classmates. Whatever feels best. This isn't set in stone, no one has to ever see this list, and people can always move from group to group as things evolve for your friend. This step will help your friend ground herself in who is important to share information with, and who is not.

WHAT are the key messages for each group? Go through each group, and let your friend decide what level of information she'd like to share with each group. Then, help her prepare the key messages. For example, to family, your friend may want to say, "I love you. I know you love me. I'll tell you when anything happens. Otherwise, prayers are fine." To co-workers, your friend may want a slightly different message: "This is what's going on and I'd love some support in this." Something important to put into this key message for each group will be the WHEN and WHERE below. This helps align and create clear expectations between your friend and her groups.

WHEN will she communicate with each group? Help your friend decide a frequency that feels safe for her. Once a week? Once a month? A one time time update? Assume all is well and that she will share only when there's big news to share? This step will allow your friend to control the timing of her messages as well as set expectations for when people will hear from her.

WHERE will your friend communicate with each group? Does your friend blog? Does she love talking on the phone? Does she usually text? Does she spend lots of time on Facebook or Instagram? This is when you'll have to use your instincts and knowledge of your friend's habits to help her navigate ways to communicate with each group. Perhaps each group can have a point of contact for your friend. Or, there can be a CaringBridge account everyone can access. Or, the CaringBridge access can be limited to those with a password. Will your friend, her caregiver, you or someone else be responsible for updates? This step allows your friend to set the tone and tenor of the communications, and to communicate in a way that feels least burdensome to her. It is important here not to push your own communication style on your friend. Let her take the lead on what feels safest to her.

WHY does your friend needs to communicate? This will probably be the hardest question to answer. You've got to break through all the social conditioning we have: to always be pleasant and only share positive information with people. Help your friend determine what the end goal is of communicating with each group. Just because your friend is learning new information about her crisis, does that create an obligation to spread that new information? Maybe. Maybe not. Hold space for this. It will really help your friend see through to who she *must* communicate with, and who she *can* communicate with.This step will give your friend the power to say: "this person/these people are — or are not — part of my team."

HOW can you help your friend implement her plan? Now that you all have a plan in place, find out how you can best support your friend in the implementation of her plan. Will you take over some of the communication duties? Perhaps you can post to a CaringBridge site for her. Will she need a little hand-holding when she tells her mom that she will only provide updates when something big happens? How can you support that experience? This step gives you the opportunity to offer up your expertise, as a friend, to smooth over situations, take on challenges, or just provide loving support.

To help make this process as easy as possible for you and your friend, I've created a template that you can use to create your friend's crisis communication plan. You can find this **free** resource online at: jennmcrobbie.com.

Keep in mind, you don't have to write out this communication plan. But, if your friend is tactile (or you are), then by all means, write it all down. It might give you and your friend something to refer back to when things really hit the fan. It might give you something you can point out to your friend when she loses her focus and can't find her way. If the idea gives your friend hives, you can write it out, and then have a burning ceremony to keep the information just between the two of you. Whatever works. But preparing the communication plan not only gives you insight into the stressors your friend might be facing, it also gives you quality time together. There is no more bonding time than the time you'll take to talk about things that are safe, and things that are not. You're helping your friend develop her own permission slip to face this crisis in her own way.

When A Communication Plan Isn't Enough

Of course, there's always the possibility that you will broach the topic of a communication plan with your friend and she'll look at you like you've grown a second head. Or, you can't even get in touch with your friend in order to begin a communication plan. After all, a communication plan does require… well… *communication*. When your friend isn't responding to multiple attempts of contact from you, then what?

You can assume, if you haven't heard from your friend in awhile, that this is an opportunity to find out where *your* boundaries are. Hopefully, you'll also find out where your friend's boundaries are, if you haven't already. Knowing your limits is probably something that we should all know, regardless of a crisis. But, crisis can make anyone act a little differently or outside of their norms. I mean, the title of this book starts with "Why is She Acting So Weird?" As long as you act with kindness, you may get a chance to enhance your friendship and establish healthy boundaries with your friend.

I cannot stand talking on the phone. I mean, I absolutely abhor it. It drives Craig nuts because I don't even want to call a pizza place to order pizza. The invent of online ordering might have saved our marriage. Despite that, I picked up the phone a lot after I was diagnosed. It seemed easier for me to talk about stuff because I was getting direct feedback. It also made me feel more connected to people. So, a new trend was born for me. I started talking to my sister, my friends, my family, on the phone a lot more. Over time, however, I started to get a little frustrated with people that I called all the time, but that didn't call me. I was especially hurt that Amy rarely called me. This all came to a head for me during several conversations that revealed just how far we'd drifted apart.

My recollection is a little hazy, but I have very distinct memories of calling her once and hearing her say to me, "Oh. I was *wondering* when you were going to tell me about that." *Guilt. Shame.* I felt like the worst friend in the world. But that quickly shifted. *Anger. Frustration.* If she was wondering how I was doing, why didn't she just reach out and ask? *Confusion. Angst.* Wait … how did she even know about what I was trying to tell her? I realized I'd put some updates on Facebook. But Amy didn't have a Facebook account. Then it dawned on me: in lieu of reaching out to me directly, Amy was using other friends' profiles on Facebook to check in on what I was doing.

I was hurt. I had no idea what to make of this. The more riled up I got, the more I realized that I just didn't have the emotional capacity to keep reaching out, if an emotional roller coaster was going be on the other side. So, I stopped reaching out.

In hindsight, I suspect that Amy was just trying to give me space. She understood that things were beyond tough for me. She understood that it would be hard to talk about things over and over. She wasn't sure what to do. So, she waited for me to tell her what to do. And when I failed to do that, she went in search of information in the only way she knew how. What she didn't understand is that she crossed some boundaries by doing that — which were boundaries that I didn't even know I had. Although I am quite open on Facebook, for example, I intend that information to be part of a mutual exchange of information. By using other friends' accounts to eavesdrop on what I was posting, I felt like I was being stalked.

More simply, what I needed was to be reminded that she wanted to hear from me.

When I was doing all the calling, I felt like a constant Debbie Downer. Eventually, I felt like I *had* to tell her what was up, and like it was an obligation, not something that served either of us or our friendship. I wanted to *want* to tell her, but even that began to fade over time. I feel selfish writing that. It feels selfish to not acknowledge that she was probably at a loss for what to do or say. But if I'm really honest, I believe that I had a right to be a little selfish. And part of that selfishness was a strong desire to have my friends tell me they thinking about me, and that they were at the ready to talk whenever I was ready. I didn't want them beating down my door at all hours of the day, but I wanted to know they'd be there, waiting. Had I been more communicative, I might have avoided a lot of the angst between Amy and me.

Amy wasn't the only friend I would stop communicating with, though. There were many times during my crisis when all I wanted to do was bury my head in the sand. I just wanted everything to go away. Or for my mind to be quiet for just one moment. Because I'm an outgoing person, it surprises some people when I need to be away from folks to recharge. The gold in my friendships is mostly in how my friends handle my silence. So, there's a little lesson in here, I think, about accepting and understanding who your friend *is*, and how *they* communicate, in crisis or not.

My friend Carrie handles my silences so very well. When I drop off the face of the planet and we haven't talked for awhile, I'll get a sweet little text from her, "I miss you." Simple. Three words. There's no request to get together or request to call or, really, any request at all. It's a simple statement of her feelings to me. It makes me feel connected to her, to hear how she is feeling. And, interestingly enough, it makes me want to tell her how I am feeling. This simple text almost always results in a dialogue or plans to get together, no matter what's going on in either of our lives.

So, the simple answer is to your friend's silence is to just reach out. And reach out with the intent of letting your friend know they are loved and thought about. *Don't add to the list of things your friend feels like she has to do.* After all, it is infinitely more important that you tell your friend how *you* are than for you to find out how *they* are. Your friend needs a break from her crisis. From thinking about herself all the time.You can help her do that by letting her think about you for awhile. It will do you both some good.

If you are at a loss for words or have trouble thinking of something to say, don't forget about the examples I have on my website: jennmcrobbie.com. You might find one that works for you, or maybe just reading will nudge your own inner communicator.

The more complicated answer, however, lies in you revealing true vulnerability. In admitting that the reason you need to hear from your friend is because you need her. There is nothing that I love more than hearing that I am loved and needed. It's a warm feeling that I carry with me everywhere I go. And when someone stops communicating, you have an opportunity to really show them how you feel. An amazing example comes from my friend Stacey. Stacey is one of those friends that I have intermittent contact with. But whenever we are together, it is like no time has passed. I consider this a mark of true friendship: when physical time passing is irrelevant to the closeness of your bond.

For this type of friendship, it's a little harder to know when one of us has "ghosted" since we aren't in touch all that often. Stacey sent me several e-mails over the course of several months. I remember reading her e-mails and thinking that I needed to reach out, but something always stopped me. I think it was fear of having to spill my guts one more time. Fear of all the emotions that were trapped inside of me. Fear of being truly vulnerable with someone. It is so much easier to face a crisis when you've hardened your exterior and just "keep marching" toward whatever the end goal is. I don't know. At any rate, Stacey finally had enough of my futzing around and sent me an e-mail that drew me right out of my silence. I'm reprinting it in its entirely here because it so beautifully illustrates both vulnerability and standing firm in boundaries:

Subject: hello, is this thing working?

Let me just say honestly that I have had enough of not hearing from you!! Yup, I am being pushy, but darn it I miss you and I feel like this whole cancer journey for you has placed a wedge.

Does that sound very selfish? Oh my goodness it does!! But I also just want to make sure you know I am there for you at any time and just generally want to make sure you are "ok", and see if you need a kick in the rear!!
:)

Thinking of you and family, ok.

S.

I responded back to that e-mail the moment I read it. So, there had been a dearth of communication between us for months, and this e-mail spurred an immediate response from me. Why? Well, Stacey let me in on how she was feeling. She was honest and a little humorous. She gave me a way out. At no time did she put an ultimatum on me (respond or else). However, she did charge me with letting her know if I needed a kick in the rear. And, in fact,

I DID need a kick in the rear. I needed a kick in the rear to respond to her. So I did.

And we never spoke of this again. Seriously. It's not like the next time we saw each other we rehashed how she dragged me out of my silence. Well, that actually might not be true. I think I might have thanked her. I hope I told her how much I appreciated her honesty and humor and vulnerability. Whether I did or I didn't, we dropped the topic. There was no guilt. No shame. No secrecy. Not from either of us. It was so refreshing to continue on with our friendship without fear that I had irreparably damaged our relationship by not responding. Stacey understood things were tough. And she took me to task for not including her. Stacey gave me gift: the gift of knowing that I was valuable to her and needed. I will treasure that gift forever.

So, when you're at the beginning of a lull in communication with your friend, you might be able to draw them out with a concrete thing to talk about, like the communication plan, if that fits in with their caregiver. If not, then a little vulnerability never hurt anyone. It can be simple — or more complex. But either way, let your friend know you need her. Let her know she's wanted, especially when she's so full of needing other people all the time. This will bring you closer. She'll know that you won't abide by not being in her life — and you'll know she wants to be in your life. You'll both love being appreciated and needed. But, remember that it's so important to check the tone of your message. No ultimatums. No fear. No guilt. No shame. Just a friend wondering how things are.

All that being said, she still might not accept your help when you offer it. And there's a very good reason why: *because sometimes accepting help means admitting that you just might need it.*

Chapter Eight:
Learning The Mathematics
Of Friendship

Sometimes being a friend means mastering the art of timing. There is a time for silence. A time to let go and allow people to hurl themselves into their own destiny. And a time to prepare to pick up the pieces when it's all over.
~ Octavia Butler

It was hard for me to accept help from people. I obviously did, as illustrated in Chapter Five. But, what I didn't tell you then, was how difficult it was to accept that help from anyone: family, friends, acquaintances. I understood that people, especially friends, wanted to help. I understood that my friends wanted to alleviate the burdens that they knew I was carrying around. I understood that they wanted to bring some joy into my life. And, they did. *Most certainly*. But that didn't make it any easier to accept their help.

Every time someone sent or dropped off a gift or a meal or a love note, I felt so *indebted* to them. They'd taken time out of their busy lives to acknowledge what was going on with me. It was overwhelming. When friends began taking on my duties, like driving my one of my daughters to preschool, I felt like I was a fraud. When I really think about it though, I would have reacted pretty similarly whether I was in a crisis or not. After all, I am a confident, independent, strong woman. I don't need other people's help, right? Except that I do. And when I accept it, the perfectionist in me rears her ugly head and says, "You're too dependent on others, Jenny."

So, that's the landscape you're dealing with before there's even a crisis in your friend's life. Then, something big and bad happens. Cancer for me. Could be a divorce for your friend. Could be the death of a loved one. Could be anything. But no matter what the crisis is, all of the normal rules change. The way you interact changes. The natural hesitation you feel when accepting help is magnified. When your friend doesn't seem to be accepting any help from you (or maybe from anyone else), you may need to take a step back and evaluate the type of help you're offering. In general, when you offer help, you're either offering to *add* things to your friends life or *take* things away. In one instance, you'll need to push your friend to accept the help. In the other, you'll need to understand the deeper psychological responses before you can proceed.

Help As Addition

Reverend Mary was the queen of adding things to my life during my crisis. She was always there, hovering just outside my peripheral vision. Although she wasn't involved in the daily "process" of my diagnosis and treatment, I always knew she was there, ready to help at a moment's notice. Probably the largest role she played in my crisis, though, was to strongly encourage me to accept help. Remember, she was the one the convinced me to post about my experience on Facebook? She was always encouraging me to act just beyond my comfort zone.

I mentioned in Chapter Five that Reverend Mary arranged for meals to be delivered to us from church members. What I didn't tell you, though, was that she had been asking Craig and I to accept meals from the church for months. Each time we'd see each other, or e-mail, or text, or talk on the phone, she would ask me if I was ready to accept help yet. I always answered, "Not yet. We're fine." It felt so awkward to me. I didn't want people who I didn't even know helping me. That just seemed like a special brand of weakness. A brand I did not want to associate with. Certainly there were others who needed help more than us. But Reverend Mary continued to ask.

One time, I gave her a long explanation about how much Craig enjoys cooking and how it gives him something to keep his mind off of what I was going through. She nodded her head. I thought I had deftly avoided saying yes. But as soon as I sent out an e-mail with the details of my chemotherapy schedule, Reverend Mary jumped right on it: "Since your chemo starts on Wednesday, I will set up meals for your family for the following Friday, Sunday, Tuesday and Thursday."

We bowed our heads to her firmness. It was clear that this was one of the ways she was going to help. And she wasn't going to let us get out of it. And she was *right*. What we didn't expect was that receiving the meals would be so heartwarming for us. That the addition of other people into our tradition of preparing meals together would be so rewarding. All the things I was worried about when Reverend Mary was asking if we would accept meals didn't come to fruition. It wasn't awkward when people came to drop off the meals. They didn't linger longer than I would have liked. Even when the meals were something that we didn't love to eat, the love of the preparer overrode our taste buds. People wrote personal little notes or just instructions on how to heat up the meal. Love expressed through the common desire to make sure that someone in pain has sustenance. How can you ask for greater help? The meals *added* to our time together. They *added* to the things we had to talk about that were not cancer-related. They *added* to our lives in immeasurable ways.

So, the thing about helping people by *adding* to their day — it's *not* a subtraction from their own life. Well, it might be in the strictest sense of the term, because the time they spent helping could have been spent doing something else. True. However, it's clear that the gift of giving actually extends to the giver. I always thought it was a bunch of bunk that giving is just as great as receiving. Until I experienced this. Until I got to see how grateful my friends and acquaintances were, when I allowed them to help me.

If the help you're offering your friend is an addition to their day or daily routine, then push your friend to accept it. Reverend Mary didn't give me an out. She pushed until I capitulated. Keep in mind, though, that these principles are tied fairly closely to the idea of doing something simple discussed in Chapter Five. You don't have to buy your friend a new car if they totaled theirs. You don't have to cover their mortgage payment if they are on disability. Just do something simple, something that you would love not to worry about if you were in their shoes.

And if your friend won't accept that help — then, keeping in mind the idea of *adding*, gently push them to accept it. If your friend won't accept a meal plan, they will (I promise) accept a meal that you bring over to their house at 4 pm before the kids get home from school. They will accept you raking their leaves or shoveling their driveway if you just show up and start working. Yes. They might protest. But they will be so appreciative. And you'll be giving them the chance to observe how happy it makes you to be allowed to help. And that will deepen your friendship well beyond this crisis. Gentle pushing when your friend is wrong shows your friend that you are the type of person that won't let your friend miss an opportunity. It shows your friend that you care so much about her that the mere act of seeing her happy makes you happy.

Help As Subtraction

However, when the type of help you're offering is *taking away* a task that your friend would normally do on her own, it gets a little more complicated. An example of subtraction is offering to take your friend's kids for a weekend. Or taking on all of your friend's duties at work. Basically, it's taking duties away from your friend so that she has more time to cope with whatever is going on in her life. And that is the *intent*, I know. The intent is to give your friend the time and space to cope with all of her struggles. Or, to just take a break from any kind of struggle and relax a bit. But, your friend may not see it that way because, when your friend is given an opportunity to slow down and smell the roses, so to speak, the roses don't always smell as fragrant as she'd hoped. Lessening your friend's workload forces her to notice the change that's going on in her life. And that opens the door to accepting the real possibilities about how life is going to change completely once this crisis is over. And that can be a lot to handle.

For me, the main "subtraction" request was to take my kids off my hands. Essentially everyone I know offered to take my kids at some point. And my first reaction, I won't lie, was anger. Thinking back on those requests now, my heart starts to palpitate a little bit. My mouth goes sort of dry and I feel a sense of panic rising in my stomach. I think of my children's faces and it makes me a little melancholy. I would immediately jump to the thought, "What makes them think that I can't take care of my own kids?" Then I would jump to, "Don't they know that my kids are what I'm fighting for? Don't take that away from me." Finally, I would settle on, "Oh, they're so crazy, I can't ask that level of help from anyone." I never really showed my anger. Or told anyone about it. Instead, I'd offer platitudes: "Thank you, but it's nice having them around." "Thank you, but I wouldn't wish them on anyone." "Thank you, but they're really not difficult."

But here's what was really going on in my head: every time someone offered to take my kids, for any length of time, it forced me to think about the fact that there might be a day when I wouldn't be able to take care of them. It forced me to go to that dark place that I've never really acknowledged, even to this day. Behind a major illness, like cancer, there is a deep sadness and fear. What you don't talk about — *can't talk about* — is your own mortality. Your own death. It's the ultimate in not being able to take care of my family, right? I couldn't even begin to contemplate it. So, I covered it up with other emotions. I wrapped myself in my kids and their routine to cover up the wound inside. To try and bring warmth to that dark, cold place inside of me.

It may sound dramatic that a request to take my kids off my hands for awhile made me think about my own death. I'll admit that it's a new revelation to me that my own mortality is what drove my insane response to people's very kind requests. I often tell people that it never crossed my mind that I would die from cancer. That's not entirely true, though, because there were times that I did think about it. Heck, there were times that that was all I thought about. Certainly not productive, but what can you do about your own thoughts, right? You can't really escape your own mortality when you're faced with the unpredictability of cancer.

Looking back now, I realize that a lot of the anger and frustration and fear I felt came from that little place in my subconscious that wanted to acknowledge my own mortality. I coped with feeling that things were happening to me that were outside of my control by really clamping down on the things I *could* control. I'd stuff that fear down into the dark recesses of my mind. To avoid thinking about it, I'd just start in on how great my kids are, or how I didn't need help with them, or how my mom would be sad if she wasn't the one to take care of the kids. I made up excuses to cover how I was really feeling. Because I didn't *want* to feel it. I didn't want to think about it. And I wasn't going to let there be a moment in time where I could sit quietly with that thought, because it might just break me in two. I wanted my home life to stay on routine. I wanted to continue doing the things that I had done before I was sick. So, whenever people offered to take my kids so that I would have time to myself, I would immediately dismiss the requests because I couldn't cope with having time to myself. I didn't want to be alone with my thoughts.

The thing about your friend accepting help that is *subtracting* from their duties is that it is, in essence, an admission that they're not at your best. It's admitting vulnerability. It's giving in to the fact that things aren't the same, and they may never be the same again. That's a lot to deal with on top of just the logistics of dealing with a crisis. There's a lot of emotional baggage that gets dragged around and up and down during a crisis, and the last thing your friend wants to do is make that burden heavier. So, they want a routine. They want things to appear normal. They want life to go on. Because then they can pretend, even if it's just for a moment, that things aren't fully upside down and turned around on their head.

When your friend is ready, she will tell you when she needs you to take a duty away. Like when I let my friends drive one of my daughters to preschool. Even though I enjoyed the duty of driving my daughter to preschool, having that duty removed from my roster was a welcome distraction from the "other" worries I had, like the ones about catching the flu while I was immunosuppressed, or scaring my daughter's classmates with my bald head. In fact, once I began to accept "subtraction" help, it became easier for me to do so. Another friend at the preschool took all of my monthly classroom duties. I'd had time, at this point, to understand that she was offering me time, not to wallow in my fear, but to focus on the future. To focus on the light at the end of the tunnel.

So, when your friend won't accept your offer of help, please don't immediately be offended. Realize that you have an opportunity here. You have an opportunity to *act* anyway — by adding something to your friend's day. Obviously don't just *act* on the subtractive offer to take her kids away for the weekend, as this is generally considered kidnapping and mostly frowned upon. But, you can use this as an opportunity to *think* about why your friend isn't accepting your offers of help. You have an opportunity to realize that the duties your friend is clinging onto might actually be saving your friend from falling down a deep dark hole of despair. Be thankful that your friend has something to distract her from those thoughts. Because those thoughts aren't helpful to anyone.

Even when you have the best of intentions, though, you might feel a distance starting between you and your friend. You might start to wonder what's happening to your friendship. You might wonder if this crisis has driven a wedge too wide to repair. At its core, though, when you feel your friend pulling away from you, it is just another opportunity to evaluate the value you both bring to each other.

Chapter Nine:
Knowing When To Hold 'Em
And When To Fold 'Em

We call that person who has lost his father an orphan; and a widower that man who has lost his wife. But that man who has known the immense unhappiness of losing a friend, by what name do we call him? Here every language is silent and holds its peace in impotence.

~ Joseph Roux

After I stopped reaching out, Amy started doing things like dropping off homemade snacks at my door when I wasn't home. I always encouraged her cooking because, to me, food brings people together. So, imagine my surprise when I find these beautiful little raspberry scones in a little bag at my doorstep. I can't recall exactly, but I have a faded memory that at first glance I had no idea who had left them. I have some sense that she must have put a little note in the bag, because I remember recognizing her handwriting before reading any of the words. The scones tasted sweet, but I felt bitter.

I know that in Chapter Five I told you that simple things, like dropping off unexpected gifts, are perfect when you don't know what to do. Most of the time, something that simple works; but by this time, it was too late. A little gift wasn't going to restore that connection again. That connection that led us to become friends in that bar, oh so many years ago. That connection that seemed so effortless. And to be honest, I had no idea how we were going to connect again like that. Every little gift or reminder that she was "out there" just served to throw me in to the guilt, shame, anger, frustration cycle. I knew I'd retreated from her, and I felt terrible about it, because being distant from her felt good. *It felt free.*

I've wracked my brain for what *she* could have done to change the result. I've wracked my brain for what *I* could have done to change the result. Maybe I'm dating myself by quoting "The Gambler" but it's so fitting: when you feel your friend pulling away from you, "you've got to know when to hold 'em and know when to fold 'em."

When To Hold 'Em

There's a group of ladies that I know that I call "my breast cancer ladies." They all had various forms of breast cancer long before I did. They were the people that I turned to when I first got my diagnosis. There was so much love and help among that group. But as I look back over our correspondence, I notice something. I notice that the responses got thinner and fewer and farther from each other. In the beginning, it was a flurry. Then, it trickled. Then, it stopped. Upon close examination, I realized that I was the one who stopped responding.

I can't think of any particular reason why I didn't respond to their inquiries after my health — mental and physical. I'm sure my selfishness reached an all time high during chemo and radiation treatments. Between not having energy and not having desire, it's not surprising that I sort of fell off the face of the planet. When this happened before I got sick; when I realized I'd pulled away from my friends, either intentionally or unintentionally, I would be ashamed. And embarrassed. I would spend all this time wishing that I hadn't stopped responding and then continued to not reach out. But things are different now. *I'm different now.* I understand that my absence, my silence, doesn't have to be a sticking point in a friendship. The true strength of these types of friendships lies in the spaces in between.

There are two key factors in friendships that can pick up where they left off: (1) friends who can stay in their own business and (2) friends who can hold space for a return.

I'm sure that when I stopped responding to e-mails and letters and telephone calls, there were some hurt feelings. When you pour out your love to someone and they don't return it, that can really hurt! But even when you have that dull ache in your heart, you have to realize that the pain you feel is yours alone. Your friend didn't cause that pain by not responding. You caused that pain by thinking you deserved a response.

What does that even mean? Let me take a little diversion here and introduce to you the idea that your *thoughts* are what makes things painful for you — or anyone else — not the *circumstances* we often find ourselves in. In *The Happiness Trap*, Russ Harris discusses the difference between *thinking* and *observing*. The "thinking self," Harris states, "is the part of you that thinks, plans, judges, compares, creates, imagines, visualizes, analyzes, remembers, daydreams, and fantasizes." The "observing self," on the other hand, "is the part of you that is responsible for focus, attention, and awareness."[xv]

If that makes full sense to you — kudos! I find it all slightly confusing. My best example of this concept of thoughts versus circumstances is chemotherapy. Before every chemo treatment, I was nervous. How was it going to be? Was it going to hurt? Was I going to have an allergic reaction? Were there going to be people there that reminded me of just how bad it could be? I'd spend days fretting over what might be. This situation represents, completely, my thoughts. There's no actual physical pain. Regardless, I'm whipping myself into frenzy based on what I'm thinking might or could or might never happen during a chemo treatment.

Meanwhile, my observing self would take over during an actual treatment. I'd observe the people around me: I'd see how they were reacting, I'd tune into how I was feeling. If I felt an inkling of a "weird" feeling, I'd let the nurse know. I didn't fret over feeling something funky or not. Nope. I'd just live, in the moment, feeling whatever I felt as it arose.

Likewise, you're hurt because your friend hasn't responded to any of your attempts to reach out. And you're *not wrong* — you do deserve to have your love returned to you! But when someone is facing a crisis, they are often like a horse with blinders on. All they can see is the lane on the track in front of them. They can't see the audience. And even if they can hear the audience, it's so cacophonous that it's hard to distinguish individual voices from the din.

When you can stay in your own business, you offer only that which makes *you* feel good. It's not about reciprocity. It's about doing something because it makes you happy. That's staying in your business. You should still do all the things that you would normally do. Cheer, if it makes you feel good to cheer for your friend. Drop off a present, if it makes you feel good to drop something at their door. But, don't do those things with the intention of eliciting a response out of your friend. If you do, then if your friend disappears for awhile — because that's what feels good to them — your feelings will be hurt. Wouldn't it feel much better to rest assured that you've done your best to keep the friendship up and running? If so, then you can be content with the silence. Content with the absence. You don't have to *like it*. But you can cope with it.

In addition to staying in your own business, strong friendships consist of lots of space. This is slightly different than the space that you held based on Chapter Two. This time, the space you hold is more like holding a reservation at a restaurant. It's like holding a seat at the table. You know there's a possibility your friend won't show. So, instead of letting that derail you, you go ahead and order dinner and start eating. If your friend shows up, you welcome her with love and excitement and happiness. You don't even need to offer a word about their absence other than, "I missed you."

Martha Beck describes the periods of intense loneliness in our lives as elevator emptying.[xvi]

Basically, the premise is that our lives are like one long elevator ride. Our growth and movement and change are represented by the many floors an elevator can stop at. As we change floors in our lives, other people will get on and off our elevator. The bad news is, some of the people we've been riding with for awhile might be getting off at the next stop. The good news, though, is that each new floor brings about opportunities for new people to get on.

I like to use this metaphor to describe the ebb and flow of friendships. Imagine your life as an elevator ride. In general, you're looking to move up from one "floor" (or phase or stage) to another. Sometimes, your elevator stops at a floor and is filled with people. You're surrounded and cocooned on the trip to the next floor. But, when the elevator stops at the next floor, some people inevitably get off. Some people stay on the elevator for several floors. Others might get back on the elevator on a different floor. But, often, the floor you get off on is the floor you stay on. As such, your elevator is going to constantly empty and fill. You have the choice of enjoying the time with the people on your elevator while they're on it, or whiling away the time fretting about their imminent departure.

My "breast cancer ladies," and indeed, many other friends in my life, inherently understand this principle. They provide all the love and compassion and joy they can when they can, because the opportunity may not come up again. They understand that the elevator might stop at their floor at any moment. And when it does, they get off the elevator with a wave and a smile. You're left feeling better and more full because of your contact with them. Sure, you might be sad that they're no longer around for the ride, but your elevator continues to move, nonetheless.

There is a time during your journey where you'll be between floors. No one new is getting on the elevator and no one old is getting off. Or, everyone may have exited at the last floor, and you're all alone. These times can be challenging. They can be lonely. But, if you understand that making it to the next level means the doors to the elevator will open to smiling faces ready to board, the time seems to pass more quickly. Sometimes those faces look familiar, like with my "breast cancer ladies." Other times, they're all new faces. But, either way, this life journey isn't one to be taken alone.

When To Fold 'Em

When you just can't let the silence ride, you run the risk of abruptly ending the friendship. It's like hitting the stop button on the elevator and prying the doors open. My friendship with Amy ended abruptly with me walking out of her house, both of us in tears. I walked out the door and got in my car. I looked back at the house before I pulled away and saw that she'd already closed the door. It wasn't just metaphorical. The door was closed. There were a few e-mails after that ... cleaning up the remnants, so to speak. But that was it.

Looking back now, I can see the pattern. The beginning of the end was when Amy didn't set up a good support system for herself. That put pressure on me, and fear in her heart. That fear led her to tell me she couldn't lose me. That fear also kept her from offering support to herself, and paralyzed her from acting when I needed her most. There were so many opportunities where we both could have stepped in and short-circuited the folding of our relationship. But it all passed too quickly, and we had our eyes closed to the possibility. As a result, we let each opportunity slip right past us.

Sometimes a friendship reaches a critical point, and there just isn't any more to do. Recognizing when this happens, and gently letting go of the relationship, is what it means to know "when to fold 'em." It means it's time to walk away. Before I go any further in describing when it's time to "fold 'em," I feel compelled to stress that this little section is *not* the point of this book! I don't want you to think that I've walked you through this path only to tell you that your friendship isn't going to make it. Because I don't believe that. The vast majority of my friendships are stronger because of my crisis. But, that being said, I do want you to know that it's a possibility. And that it happened to me and Amy. I wasn't ok with that for a long time, but I'm getting there. And I want you to feel ok about it if this happens in your life.

There are times when you're going to have to get off your friend's elevator, or they have to get off yours, knowing that this is the end of your journey together. How do you know when it's that time? Well, the clearest sign lies in you — in the friend who is not in a crisis. If your fear has reached such a crescendo that you find yourself ignoring the changes that your friend is going through and requiring her to "stay the same," then that is a sign that it may be time to fold 'em. When you truly can't accept the changes that are happening, it is actually more likely to preserve your friendship if you step away.

Martha Beck calls this type of behavior a "Change Back Attack."[xvii] The idea is that whenever people undergo a major change, that the change sort of ripples out from them (the reverse of the Ring Theory discussed in Chapter One). Any person that's been in contact with your friend will be forced to recognize the shifts, and may need to alter their expectations or actions as a result. Not everyone is ok with this type of change. Not everyone is ok with changing just because someone else is changing. And when you're not ok with changing, then you want everything to go back to the way that it was. You want your friend to "change back" so that you don't have to incorporate the new shifts into your friendship.

Martha writes about Change Back Attacks from the perspective of the "attackee." From the perspective of the person who has done all the changing, and finds themselves confronted by people who don't support their change. She suggests putting together a "systematic defense" to the attack. But, what if you're the attacker? What if you're the one seeking to change your friend *back* to the way she was? What if you're looking to preserve the beautiful friendship that you have built and that this change is now threatening? If you engage in a battle with your friend, even if you win the battle, you'll lose the war.

Why will you lose the war? Well, even if you win the battle to change your friend back, there's likely to be a lot of resentment in your friendship as a result. In the context of your friend, a lot of the changes she's undergone have not been because she wanted to change. Nope. The crisis has *forced* those changes. So, when you force her to go back to the way she was, you're asking her to not recognize the profound nature of her crisis. If you lose the battle to change your friend back, you still lose the war because you have already drawn a line in the sand: *I don't like the changes and I can't cope with them.*

You both lose. So, sometimes at this point, it's better to just set your friendship free. It's time for you to get off your friend's elevator. Or, if you prefer to think of it this way, it's time for your friend to get off of your elevator. If it's meant to be, your paths will cross again. If it's not meant to be, you can be confident that you stood firmly on your own ground, protecting both your interests and your friend's interests. You don't always have to agree with your friend's changes. That doesn't mean it's not going to hurt. It *will* hurt. And you'll be sad. But if you can part ways with love in your heart and a smile on your face, then you don't have to stare at a closed door as you drive away. Instead, you can, even with tears in your eyes, wish them well as they continue on their journey.

Conclusion

True Friendship is like sound health;
the value of it is seldom known until it is
lost.
~ *Charles Caleb Colton*

I have gained and strengthened many friendships, too many to name and only a few of whose names appear in this book. And I have lost, too. I still love Amy. I always will. But that doesn't mean that I'm ready to be friends again. Or ever, for that matter. And I'm actually ok with that. I hope you are too. It's hard to hear about the ending of any friendship. You always want to know what could have been done to stop it.

This book is the culmination of that process for me. I hope you feel a sense of completion like I do. I hope you see how I was wrong at times. But, really, that's just being human, isn't it? Honestly, I wish Amy had this book at the time of my diagnosis, or that I better understood exactly how weird I was really acting. Maybe it would have made the difference. Or, maybe it was just her floor. We just wanted the best for each other and for our friendship. And as of right now, releasing the bond we had with each other is the best thing for our friendship. It feels good to release the things and people that aren't on my elevator any more. Feeling good is where I want to end this story for you.

It's been over a year since I was diagnosed with breast cancer. I can actually see the light at the end of the tunnel as the end of this year approaches. And the light is *so* bright on the other side. It's so bright that I have to squint to see what lies ahead. When I turn to see what is behind me, it's so dark I can barely see the edges of the path I've walked. But I know the path. I could traverse it with my eyes closed. And looking back carefully, it is speckled with the light of so many great friends. Don't get me wrong, I don't want to ever walk it again. But I know that if I have to, I'll be able to avoid the pot holes and scary corners that held me up on this trip.

My friendships are all very different on this side of the tunnel. They are deeper. More meaningful. More full of give and take and truth and acceptance. I feel a continuous outpouring of love. And that feeling persists, even when I'm not in direct contact with my friends. This is the residual feeling you get when someone has given you so much love. It leaves an imprint on your soul. I want you to leave your imprint on your friend's soul. I know that's a little scary and intimidating. But don't let the unknown intimidate you. You are a good friend. I know this like I know that the sky is blue. And I know this, even though I don't know you, because you've picked up this book and invested your precious time into it. Thank you. Thank you for spending your time with me. For letting me impart my experience on you.

There's another imprint on my soul, though, that's deeper than the others. It's the print left by my friendship with Amy. I embrace that footprint. I celebrate it. Because she's the one that prepared me to receive such love from others. I choose not to focus on the hurt and confusion of the last year. She was there for me in the only way she knew how. Even when I wasn't always the best friend to her, she did what she could. And our paths diverged anyway. The only lingering sadness, in all honesty, is this — I wish we could have parted ways with a hug and smile, instead of with tears and a closed door.

Tomorrow morning, I am getting on a plane with Craig and Tess and Eddie. We're going on a trip to celebrate life. To celebrate my 40th birthday. To celebrate friendship. To forge a new bond, based on surviving the tension of the last year intact. It feels like a trip full of milestones. I've talked to Tess quite a bit about this book as I've been writing it. She's been a little bit muse, a little bit supporter, and a little bit critic. The distance with Amy has been tempered by her closeness. My relationship with Tess has led me to promise, to myself, to spend more time concentrating on the people that are actually on my elevator, rather than focusing on the ones that got off on a different floor. No shame. No regret. It is infinitely better to enjoy the positive than to linger on the negative. And there is a whole lot of positive in my life to linger on. There is for you and your friend too. But sometimes it takes a crisis for anyone to really see it.

I hope this book helps you to navigate the pot holes and dark corners on your friend's journey. I hope that you end up on a plane with your friend at the end of the crisis, smiling at each other across the aisle, thinking of how lucky you are to be there with her. If you're in the middle of the crisis now, I hope that this book gives you some practical advice and instructions for how to raise the level of your friendship.

If you're the type of friend that is just preparing for the next crisis around the corner, I hope you practice the skills here. Many of them, as I've noted, are ways to be a good friend, crisis or not. I intend to practice what I've written here. Every day. And I might fail sometimes. But in that failure, I'll be given the opportunity to rise again. And it is in *getting back up when you've fallen* where friendships are strengthened and life long bonds are forged. I didn't understand that until we were all thrust into the fire of my crisis together. But now, I do. Now, I know that getting up when you fall matters. And that's how you can start to change all your friendships right this moment. Call that friend you haven't spoken to in awhile. Send an e-mail. Send a text. In fact, as I was writing this, I got a text from a friend I've known for 25 years but haven't had contact with in while. Our friendship has ebbed and flowed. But when I reached out to her about my cancer, she hopped right back on the elevator. It's not quite like it was 25 years ago ... but what is, really? It's just right for right now. It feels good to reconnect and profess our love and caring for each other. Don't wait 25 years to do that with your friends. You deserve to feel the happy I feel right this moment.

I also hope that you understand that it doesn't always work out the way you planned. I hope that you're ending this book feeling good about how you've acted, what you've said, and what you've offered to your friend. Or, that you're feeling like you know what you *can* do. Go forth and be the good friend that you are. Celebrate your weirdness. Celebrate the crisis. Celebrate the the opportunity to rise and fall, together.

"The greatest gift of life is friendship, and I have received it."
~ Hubert H. Humphrey

Acknowledgements

Even sitting here just thinking about the people I want to thank is sending me into fits of tears. I can't believe how blessed I am. I feel like I've lived a charmed life, and it's solely due to a multitude of wonderful souls who decided that they would return my undying love.

To my husband, Craig. Thank you for never once doubting me. Thank you for your steadfast love, especially during those times I felt unlovable. Not only have you always believed in me, but you've always supported me...even when I come up with some cockamamie scheme like life coach training or writing a book. Craig, your unwavering love and heartfelt honesty make life worth living.

To my children, Emma and Isla. You teach me, daily, what it means to live life fully. I love you both to Jupiter and back and back and back.

To my parents, without whom I wouldn't even exist. Mom and Dad, you taught me all sorts of things ranging from how to tie shoelaces to how to spit shine combat boots. You have always supported me and told me that I can achieve anything as long as I set my mind to it. You were right.

To my sister, Paula. You never pushed while I was writing this book, even though I know it was probably killing you inside to find out exactly what all of this was about. I'm so lucky to have been born into having a best friend. Oh — and those piggy back rides? They really did help make me stronger.

To Tess. Thank God for stroller skating and the creepy zoo!! Thank you for proving that a pure heart and positive intentions are worthwhile lifetime pursuits.

To Angela, my book coach, publisher and friend. My inner author was hiding. You taught me how to coax her out with kindness and love. This gift is immeasurable.

To all my friends - past, present and future. Please know that I love you and appreciate you. I won't always show it and sometimes I'll do and say dumb stuff. But please don't ever doubt my love.

And lastly — to cancer. I know you were just a part of me that went uncontrollably wild. I'm not sure I'll ever fully accept our time together — but I'm not angry. A whole hell of a lot of good has come to my life after you. So, thanks, I guess. You don't get the last word.

About The Author

Jenn McRobbie is a recovering Army Captain and lawyer who has found that her life long desire to "help people" is better achieved through being a life coach and speaker. Jenn worked with cancer survivors of all types long before her own diagnosis with breast cancer. Jenn hopes that her experience will enable her to positively impact the lives of survivors, their families and most importantly — with this book — their friends.

Jenn lives in Virginia with her husband, two beautiful daughters, dog and a host of friends to enjoy wine with on the front porch.

Connect with Jenn at: jennmcrobbie.com

About Difference Press

Built for aspiring authors who are looking to share transformative ideas with others throughout the world, Difference Press offers life coaches, healing professionals, and other non-fiction authors a comprehensive solution to get their book published without breaking the bank or taking years. A boutique-style alternative to self-publishing, Difference Press boasts a fair and easy-to-understand profit structure, low-priced author copies, and author-friendly contract terms.

Tackling the technical end of publishing

The comprehensive publishing services offered by Difference Press mean that your book will be designed by an experienced graphic artist, available in printed, hard copy format, and coded for all eBook readers, including the Kindle, iPad, Nook, and more. We handle all of the technical aspects of your book creation so you can spend time focusing on your business.

Over 20 years of experience nurturing books that make a difference

Founder Dr. Angela Lauria has been bringing the literary ventures of authors and personal coaches to life since 1994. You can learn more about Dr. Lauria's innovative approach to book creation or take advantage of a variety of free writing resources at:

www.TheAuthorIncubator.com

Your Delicious Book

If you're like many authors, you have wanted to write a book for a long time, maybe you have even started a book … or two… or three … but somehow, as hard as you have tried to make your book a priority other things keep getting in the way. Some authors have fears about their writing abilities or whether or not what they have to say is important enough. For others, the challenge is making the time to write their books or having the accountability to see it through to the end. It's not just finding the time and confidence to write that is an obstacle, the logistics of finding an editor, hiring an experienced designer, and figuring out all the technicalities of publishing stops many authors-in-transformation.

For more information on how to participate in our next Your Delicious Book program visit www.TheAuthorIncubator.com/delicious.

Other Books By Difference Press

Why Smart People Do Stupid Things
by Dr. Frank Stass

Radical Abundance: A Journey from
Not Enough to Plenty
by Christy Lambert

Surviving 30: Waking Up to Your True Self
Through Your Saturn Return
by Karen Hawkwood

Choosing Delight: True Life Stories of Quitting a
Soul-Sucking Job and Doing What You Love for a
Living
by Leyla Day

Own It: Powerful Speaking For Powerful Women
by Tricia Karp

Personal Alchemy: The Missing Ingredient For
Law Of Attraction Success
by Michelle Martin Dobbins

Married To A Vegan: Is It For Better Or For Worse When A Spouse Embraces Healthy Living And A Plant-Based Low-Fat Diet
by Caren Albers

Speak Up For Your Business: Presentation Secrets for Entrepreneurs Ready to Tell, Sell, and Compel
by Michelle Mazur Ph.D.

The Crowdfunding Book: A How-to Book for Entrepreneurs, Writers, and Inventors
by Patty Lennon

Thank You!

Without friends like you, this world would be a lonely place. Thank you for taking the time to read my book. Thank you for taking the time to be a friend to someone in crisis. Thank you for being willing to change to make that experience a deeper one for you and your friend.

Don't forget to go to my website: jennmcrobbie.com to access the following **free** resources:

1. **Care Messages**: for when you're at a loss for words to tell your friend you love her.
2. **You vs. I**: examples of You vs. I statements that may aid you in giving advice to your friend.
3. **Communication Plan**: a ready-made template for you and your friend to use, together.

Another Special Offer
For Readers

As a special thank you, your book purchase entitles you to 2 months of free access to my PROBLEM SOLVED Club for solving friendship related problems. Click here to sign up and find out more:

http://eepurl.com/bbJLpv

Notes

[i] Silk, Susan and Barry Goldman. "How Not to Say the Wrong Thing," Los Angeles Times, April 7, 2013.articles.latimes.com/2013/apr/07/opinion/la-oe-0407-silk-ring-theory-20130407

[ii] Cannon, Walter Bradford. Bodily Changes in Pain, Hunger, Fear and Rage. New York-London, 1915.

[iii] Levine, Peter A. Healing Trauma. Boulder, Colorado: Sounds True, Inc. 2008, 29.

[iv] McLaren, Karla. The Language of Emotions: What Your Feelings Are Trying To Tell You. Boulder, Colorado: Sounds True, Inc., 2010, 31.

[v] Moore, Alecia and Max Martin and Johan Karl Shuster. Fucking Perfect. Pink. © 2010 by LaFace Records and RCA Records. MP3.

[vi] Bolte Taylor, Jill. My Stroke of Insight: A Brain Scientist's Personal Journey. Viking, 2008.

[vii] McLaren, Language of Emotions, 30.

[viii] McLaren, Language of Emotions, 30.

[ix] Joe Navarro, "Body Language of the Hands", Psychology Today, Jan 20, 2010, accessed October

28, 2014,
http://www.psychologytoday.com/blog/spycatcher/201001/body-language-the-hands

[x] "Palm Positions," http://www.study-body-language.com/gesture.html, accessed October 28, 2014.

[xi] Brown, Brene. The Gifts of Imperfection: Let Go of Who You Think You're Supposed to Be and Embrace Who You Are. Center City, Minnesota: Hazelden, 2010, 107

[xii] Byron Katie, The Little Book: The Work of Byron Katie, An Introduction (Katie International, Inc, 2013), accessed November 12, 2014, www.thework.com/downloads/little_book/English_LB.pdf

[xiii] www.caringbridge.com. From their "about us" page, "Caring Bridge transforms your personal connections into support when you need it most. By creating a free CaringBridge website, people in a time of need can share updates, photos and videos, connecting with friends and family who care and want to help."

[xiv] Beck, Martha. Steering By Starlight. Find Your Right Life No Matter What! New York, New York: Rodale, 2008, 40-48.

[xv] Russ Harris. The Happiness Trap. Boston, Massachusetts: Trumpeter Books. 2007, 2008. iTunes/iBooks edition, chapter 7.

[xvi] Beck, Steering By Starlight, 103-104.

[xvii] Martha Beck, "The New You: Handing Change-Back Attacks," Creating Your Right Life Blog, accessed November 25, 2014, marthabeck.com/2012/10/change-back-attacks/

Made in the USA
Middletown, DE
12 February 2016